D0944521

BURGESS LEA PRESS
donates 100 percent
of our after-tax profits
to food-related causes.

BURGESS LEA PRESS
BLP
ALL PROFITS to GOOD CAUSES

ONIONS
ETCETERA

ONIONS
ETCETERA

The Essential Allium Cookbook

More than 150 recipes for leeks, scallions, garlic,
shallots, ramps, chives and every sort of onion

KATE WINSLOW AND GUY AMBROSINO

BLP

Quarto is the authority on a wide range of topics.

Quarto educates, entertains and enriches the lives of
our readers—enthusiasts and lovers of hands-on living.
www.quartoknows.com

Copyright © 2017 by Kate Winslow and Guy Ambrosino

Published in 2017 by Burgess Lea Press, an imprint of
Quarto Publishing Group USA Inc., 400 First Avenue North,
Suite 400, Minneapolis, MN 55401 USA.

Telephone: (612) 344-8100
Fax: (612) 344-8692

quartoknows.com
Visit our blogs at quartoknows.com

Burgess Lea Press titles are also available at discounts
in bulk quantity for industrial or sales-promotional use.
For details contact the Special Sales Manager at Quarto
Publishing Group USA Inc., 400 First Avenue North, Suite
400, Minneapolis, MN 55401 USA.

10 9 8 7 6 5 4 3 2 1

ISBN 978-0-9972113-1-3

Library of Congress Control Number: 2016952743

Design Jan Derevjanik
Art direction Ken Newbaker
Photography Guy Ambrosino
Production Victor Cataldo
Photo of authors by Laura Miller

Printed in China

MIX
Paper from
responsible sources
FSC® C101537

Burgess Lea Press donates 100% of after-tax publishing
profits on each book to culinary education, feeding the
hungry, farmland preservation and other food-related causes.

For Elio

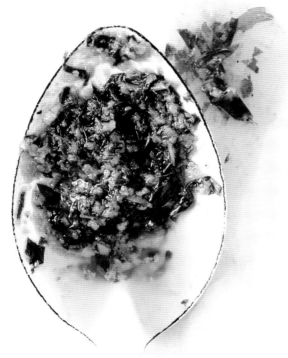

CONTENTS

6

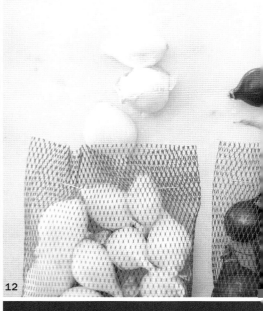

10

11

12

16

17

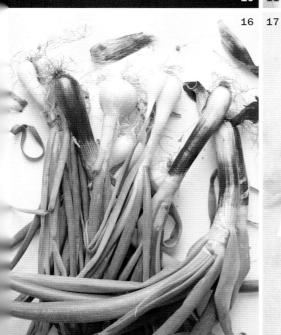

(1) YELLOW ONION
(2) WHITE ONION
(3) RED ONION
(4) SWEET ONION
(5) SCALLIONS
(6) CHIVES
(7) GARLIC CHIVES
(8) GARLIC CHIVES
(9) LEEKS
(10) SHALLOTS
(11) CIPOLLINI
(12) PEARL ONION
(13) RAMPS
(14) GARLIC SCAPES
(15) GREEN GARLIC
(16) SPRING ONION
(17) GARLIC

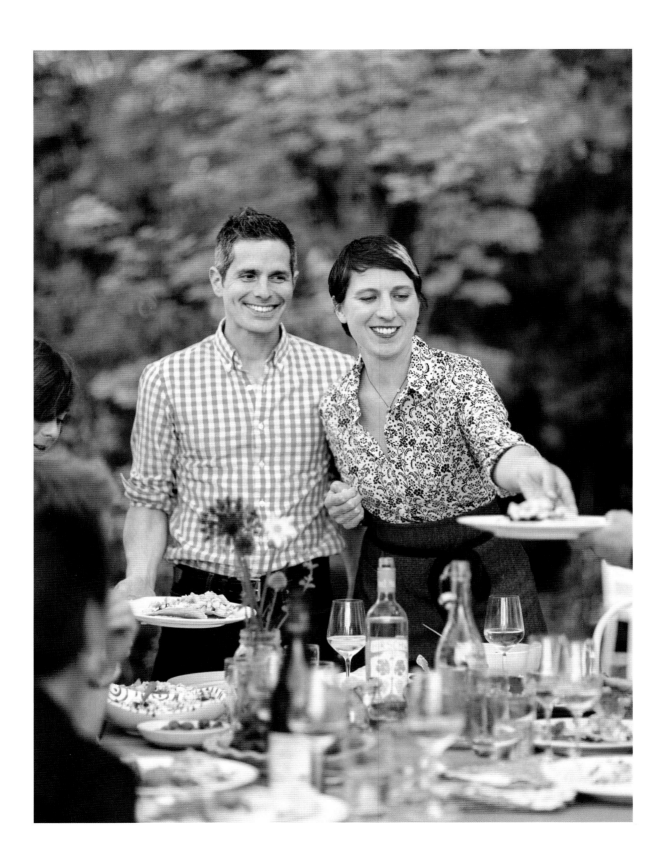

INTRODUCTION
IS THERE AN ONION
IN THE HOUSE?

SOME OF THE BEST MEALS BEGIN WITH THE folklore of the kitchen: recipes passed down through stories, laughter over the stove and sweet moments together at the table. And almost every meal begins with an onion. It has been this way since people have been cooking.

A cookbook devoted to onions-and by onions, we mean not only the hardworking yellow and red storage onions but all members of the allium family, from marble-sized pearl onions to long leeks and scallions and garlic in all its forms and stages—could include, literally, almost every savory dish known to cooks. A tiny bit daunting, to say the least. How could we find our way in? How would we narrow down what to include? As in every other aspect of our lives, we realized that the best bet was to take a step back, start small and keep it personal.

WE'VE BEEN HEARING stories of fried water for years. With laughing eyes, Guy's aunts would tell of a magical soup that their mother made when the pantry was bare. Like so many good things, it started with onions, one for each member of the family, cooked gently in olive oil until limpid and golden.

As the sliced onions sizzled quietly in the pan, the kitchen filled with their delicious perfume, drawing everyone closer, mouths watering. Once the onions had reached their sweet spot, their mother added water to make the simplest of broths. Finally, just before serving, she whisked eggs into the pan (again, one per person) to thicken the soup.

On the counter, she had lined up shallow bowls and placed a thick slice of stale bread in each and then ladled the soup over them. In the warm embrace of the fried water, the bread softened and became satisfying chewy. A perfect meal, made from little more than air. One that Guy's aunts and mother still make for themselves when feeling sick or low. We knew we needed that recipe.

So one morning, while we were smack-dab in the middle of creating this book, Guy's Aunt Aggie came down to teach us how to make fried water. Aggie is 84 years old, the mother of seven and grandmother of 30, and has the energy and sunny outlook of a well-adjusted teenager. She grew up in northern New Jersey during the Great Depression, the youngest child of a large Italian-American brood. Fried water was a staple. Aggie's husband, her older brother and his girlfriend and Guy's Aunt Patricia also came down for the day. They had all grown up eating fried water in one form or another.

It didn't really take five people to teach us how to make fried water, but it took that many to share the history of it, the recipe's background and the family memories of growing up poor but eating well. As we sat together around our table, eating lunch, this simplest of recipes took on the heft and weight of an heirloom quilt, a little bit added here, some embroidery there, flecks of color all over. Fried water is not the prettiest dish you've ever seen, but it is good. It's a wonder how a couple of onions can be combined and stretched to feed a large family, and since it was always made with love, fried water became the stuff of legend—and now, of inspiration.

HOW MANY TIMES have we stood in our own kitchen, uncertain, stomachs grumbling, the clock ticking uncomfortably close to dinner time? We pluck an onion from the pile of alliums near the stove, peel away its crackling yellow skin and begin chopping.

Yes, we're buying some time as we figure out a meal. Will this onion become a pasta sauce, a soup, a curry, a pot of beans, a salad? Who knows? It may even have the potential to become that as-yet unknown dish that stays in our son's memory forever, one that he passes down as dinner and folklore to his own children.

Onions are the surest kitchen partners we know. If there's an onion in the house, we're confident we can make something good since, with very little coaxing, it can provide such a range of flavor—from sharp and almost spicy when raw to mellow and sweet when cooked. How empty our kitchen would be without them!

ONE OF THE things we love best about onions is that, for the most part, they are accessible, available to everyone and—importantly—very affordable. While we enjoy heirloom varieties of cipolini onions and garlic, handfuls of seasonal garlic scapes and gorgeous spring onions from our farm market, we appreciate that yellow, red and white onions are a grocery store staple all year round. They are constantly in demand so the stock is always fresh and rotated.

Onions most likely originated in central Asia, in the area around present-day Iran, Pakistan and Uzbekistan, and have been grown and harvested since at least 5000 BC, making them one of the oldest cultivated plants we know. The basic ancient languages—Chinese, Hebrew, Sanskrit and Greek—each have quite distinct names for onions, so alliums were most likely present in each of those cultures during that formative time.

Much has been made of onions in Egyptian times—depictions of onions and garlic appear in many tomb wall murals, and they have been found paired with mummified remains. They were probably brought to the Americas by the Spanish, and onion seeds were certainly among the necessary goods packed by the earliest settlers.

It's fitting that the word onion comes from *unio*, which means to unite and refers to its single bulb structure, for the onion unites all the ingredients in a dish, and it's a common denominator in kitchens all over the world. Think of how an onion, leek, shallot or garlic—alone or in combination with other vegetables or spices—is the start to almost any dish you can imagine.

Consider the French mirepoix of finely diced carrots, celery and onions, the Spanish sofrito of onions, garlic and tomato, the Cajun trinity of onions, bell peppers and celery, the Chinese use of scallions, garlic and ginger, the Indian reliance on onions, garlic and ginger. And though onions and their allium cousins are so often considered a seasoning—a way to boost the meat, the grain, the other vegetable that is the star of the show—you need only think of French onion soup or flaky scallion pancakes or a big basket of crisp fried onion rings to remember that onions can be the focus of a dish, and happily so.

What other ingredient can take on both starring and supporting roles like this, slipping in and out of the forefront of dishes with confidence and grace?

THESE ARE THE recipes that we love and that mean something to us, that resonate deeply on an emotional and historical level. They are drawn from all stages of our lives, and once again, the onion shows its unifying power, popping up in dishes from childhood to last night's dinner. Turns out we, like everyone else, come from a long line of onion eaters.

Growing up, Kate spent most of her time in Pittsburgh with her brother and their busy school teacher parents who still managed to sit down together almost every night for dinner. In the winters, they often threw big parties and their

small house shook with the laughter of friends and neighbors. The biggest tradition for many years was an epic New Year's Day open house, during which all the neighbors straggled over during the day for Bloody Marys and a dining room table packed with food—spinach dip served in a bread bowl (it was the '80s, after all), platters of smoked fish, cheese and cured sausages—and then, after the neighbors left, segued into a sit-down dinner of roast pork, kielbasa and sauerkraut for two dozen close friends and relatives.

In summer, the family moved down to a remote part of the Florida Keys, trading urban gray for sunny days, starry nights, open water and hours spent fishing (or in Kate's case, complaining about fishing). Here was a welcome juxtaposition to Pittsburgh's meat and potatoes diet—fresh seafood, tropical fruit and lots of bright Cuban food.

Guy grew up in New Jersey, part of that big Italian family in which good, homemade food was paramount to every gathering and the basis of so many passionate conversations. His father owned a fish market, and Guy spent his weekends sweeping the floor of the shop, peeling shrimp and helping customers. His family still celebrates Christmas Eve with a feast of the seven fishes—a huge enterprise that involves bacala in many forms (fried, salad and in brandade), shrimp, eel, stuffed calamari, a vat of lobster sauce for the cappellini and whatever else that year's host decides to experiment with. It's just what you would dream of: noisy, chaotic and very fun.

The two of us met in New Mexico after college, when we both worked at a small weekly newspaper in Santa Fe. Guy was the staff photographer, and Kate was trying to break into journalism. We connected instantly over art, music, a shared sense of humor and certainly, food. Santa Fe is a place of artists, wanderers and dreamers from all over, and we were lucky to be there in our twenties, that magical time when you have, well, time to devote to long talks and philosophical explorations. Many of those meandering conversations took place around the kitchen table, and that is still one of

our favorite places to be. We have always loved to bring people together, especially over food.

After many years in Santa Fe, we headed back east, first to Philadelphia and later to New York City, where Kate worked as an editor at *Gourmet* magazine and where our son Elio was born. Along the way, we gathered up recipes like souvenirs, taste mementos that we filed away into our collective family recipe box. From Kate's childhood, there were her Aunt Emma's pierogi with buttery onions from Pittsburgh and the bistec palomillo, Cuban steak cooked with liberal amounts of lime juice and onions that she loved eating in the Keys.

From Guy's family came the fried water and the pizza escarole. From our time together in northern New Mexico, we collected the state's beloved red chile sauce, enchiladas and shrimp tostadas, as well as dishes from friends that were deliciously anomalous blips in the high desert, things like Korean beef short ribs and Thai cucumber salad.

During our time in Philadelphia and New York, we binged on the flavors of the Middle East, Asia and India, trekking north, south, east or west as our bellies led us, to Chinatown, Curry Hill, the further reaches of Queens and the food carts tucked on the corners of Sixth Avenue near Kate's office. But some of the very best eating happened within that highrise office in the middle of Times Square, where the food editors created and tested recipes from all over the world—what a delicious education!

And then we went to Sicily. In 2009, after several years in Manhattan and Brooklyn—where life was beginning to feel like more of a grind than a joy and there weren't nearly enough rambling dinners with friends—we decided we were ready for a change.

Kate quit her job at *Gourmet*, Guy packed up his studio, we sold our shoebox apartment in Brooklyn and grabbed hold of a hare-brained scheme to head to Sicily for a few weeks while we figured out what was next. We ended up working at the Anna Tasca Lanza School of Sicilian Cooking—Kate helping with classes, and Guy working as a photographer documenting the recipes, as well as the farm's harvests, the cheese-making and preservation techniques. Those weeks turned into months. We enrolled little Elio in the town's Catholic preschool, where the two nuns who ran the program were barely taller than their charges and spoke not a word of English.

During those special months, we learned to cook with wild fennel, still-warm sheep's milk ricotta and fresh sardines no bigger than our pinkies, but somehow it was the onions that stayed with us. Hardly any dish at Case Vecchie started without a red onion. Grown on the family's farm, these Tropea onions were about the size of a child's fist, deep purple and sweetly spicy. They were the first step in making caponata, the piquant bite in the salsa pronta, the crown on the sfincione. When the basket of onions in the kitchen ran out, we walked thirty paces across the courtyard to the jasmine-covered storeroom and cut down a new bunch hanging from the rafters.

When we returned to the States, settling into a small town along the Delaware River in New Jersey, wild fennel was but a dream, our ricotta no longer came from the shepherd up the hill, and we were back to canned sardines most of the time. But onions? Onions we could do. And we do—every day.

THE FOLLOWING RECIPES are organized according to the somewhat arbitrary way we think of alliums, but there is a method to our madness. First up are the keepers: These are the workhorses of the kitchen, the yellow, white and red storage onions that are always in our pantry and that make up the bulk of our cooking. They are the seasoning basis for soups, stocks, beans and sauces, add crunch and heat to salads, and can be cooked down to a mellow suppleness. They are, quite simply, indispensable.

Then come the sweet onions, similar in size and shape to regular storage onions but with a lower sulfur content, which means their flavor is milder and their flesh juicier. They also don't keep as well, so we use them up quickly when we get them—caramelizing, frying and stuffing them.

Scallions and chives come next, alliums that are known for their greenery, which we make good use of, both as a seasoning and a garnish. We love scallions for their fresh, snappy oniony perfume, plus they are so easy to use—no peeling! Chives are the only allium we grow in our tiny yard, and we are happy to have them in quantity so we can make creamy chive dressing and chive omelets.

Shallots and leeks are the dearest of the bunch; other than our weekly vinaigrette, for which we always keep a couple of shallots on hand, these are special purchases, and we buy them as needed. Same goes for the little guys—diminutive pearl onions and cipollini, which look like miniature flying saucers. Both are delicious in an agro-dolce—or sweet and sour—sauce or pickled. Their bite-sized nature makes them a perfect addition to stews or kebabs. They are well worth the bit of effort it takes to peel them.

In the spring, we look forward to a special run of alliums. Ramps, sometimes known as wild leeks, arrive first—a harbinger of all the good green things to come. Soon after, we start seeing the spring onions and green garlic—the green-topped fresh onions and garlic pulled to make room so that their neighbors can grow to full size. And a little later, the garlic scapes shoot up, twisting in the fields, ready to lend their gentle garlic scent and crunch to stir-fries and salsas. And finally, there is garlic, for which a single chapter only begins to scratch the surface.

WE HOPE THAT you'll find in these recipes a new appreciation for this taken-for-granted family of vegetables—and a reminder of just how bereft our kitchens would be without it. We know you have an onion or two in your own kitchen, just waiting to be turned into something delicious.

OUR ALLIUM PANTRY

WE ALWAYS HAVE A FEW POUNDS OF YELLOW AND RED ONIONS ON HAND—THEY ARE THE FIRST step of so much that we cook. Because they don't keep as well, white and sweet onions are more of a special occasion purchase, when we have a certain recipe in mind. A handful of shallots is always on the counter, ready to be minced and whisked into vinaigrette. Ditto for garlic. A bunch or two of scallions can usually be found in the fridge, and even if they're a little past their prime, we just trim the limp bits and carry on. In addition to these allium staples, here are a few other things we always have on hand:

SALT: For everyday cooking, and for most of the recipes in this book, we use coarse kosher salt. Grocery stores usually carry just two brands: Morton's and Diamond Crystal. We prefer Morton's purely for aesthetic reasons—the sturdy blue box fits neatly into our cabinets, and the metal spout makes for easy pouring. The size of the salt crystals does vary between brands, so always taste as you cook, adding a little more salt—or holding back—according to your tastes. In addition, we always keep some flaky fleur de sel close at hand for finishing dishes with a salty crunch.

BUTTER: We admit to a penchant for salted butter—we love how it tastes melting in a pool over freshly toasted bread. And even though it goes against what most cooks, books and magazines recommend, we often cook and bake with salted butter, too, simply because it's what we have on hand. We find it doesn't make a huge difference in the final dish, as long as you keep an eye on how much salt you add. More important is to use butter that is very fresh, and preferably organic. We usually keep sticks tightly wrapped in the freezer until ready to use.

OILS: The olive oil we use most often is from California Olive Ranch, a nicely flavored but still quite neutral domestic oil that is readily available at most supermarkets. We also keep on hand grapeseed oil for salad dressings, peanut oil for frying (or vegetable oil if feeding someone with a nut allergy) and toasted sesame oil for Asian dishes.

VINEGARS: We love the acidic tang of vinegars almost as much as the sweetness of alliums, and the two go so well together. Our go-to is sherry vinegar, which we appreciate for its mellow sparkle, but we also love white wine, red wine, unfiltered apple cider, aged balsamic, white balsamic and unseasoned rice vinegar, all of which are called for in these pages. There is always a gallon jug of white distilled vinegar under the sink, which we use for basic pickles, like Pickled Red Onions (page 104). We also glug it into our dishwasher before each run, to help keep the glasses clear.

DRIED SPICES: The messy spice drawer is the necessary evil of the happy cook. Ours is always a jumble of cumin (both seeds and ground), cinnamon (ground and whole sticks), coriander seeds, black peppercorns, allspice, oregano, whole cloves, nutmeg, and fennel seeds, plus all the others that you buy for one recipe and that linger around.

FRESH HERBS: How lovely summer is, when you can step outside and snip off a few sprigs of mint, rosemary or basil, as you need. The rest of the year,

it's off to the grocery store (though our thyme is incredibly hardy and often still providing even under a thin crust of snow). You'll see that many of these recipes call for combinations of parsley, mint, cilantro and dill—all easy enough to find. When we call for bay leaves, fresh ones are preferable to dried.

HOT STUFF: We love it, and keep it on hand in several forms. Easiest and most basic is the shaker of crushed red pepper flakes that we use almost daily, for seasoning pasta, pizza, veggies, sauces—anything that needs an instant, uncomplicated jolt of heat. Other dried ground chiles that we use regularly are Aleppo pepper and *gochugaru* (Korean red chile flakes), which both offer a sweet fruitiness along with the spice. There are usually a couple

of fresh jalapeños and serranos rolling around the crisper drawer, and one shelf on the fridge door houses a collection of hot sauces—nothing crazy—sriracha, Cholula, Tabasco etc. Finally, our nostalgia for New Mexico, where we used to live, means we always have plenty of roasted Hatch green chile and Chimayó red chile powder in the freezer. The pantry is usually stocked with an assortment of dried whole ancho, pasilla and New Mexico red chiles, which are indispensable when making the various spice pastes in these pages, such as Hrous (page 56), Harissa (page 300) and Romesco Sauce (page 270).

MUSTARD: We always have Dijon mustard, both smooth and grainy, on hand. We like the sharpness of Maille, and can eat it by the spoonful.

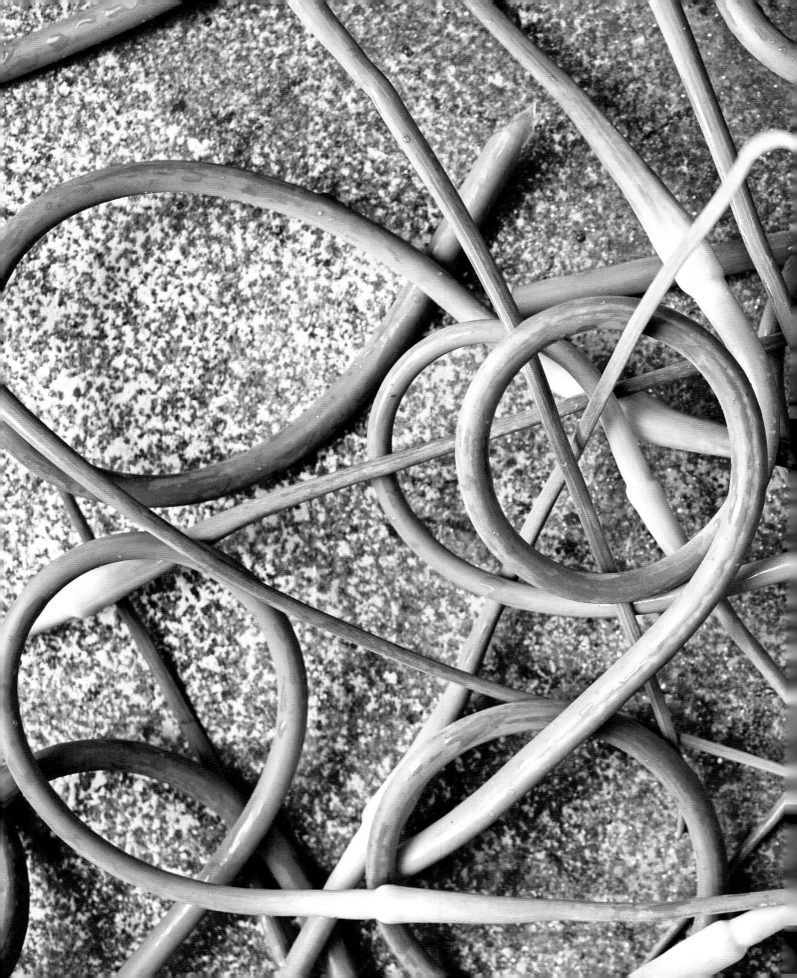

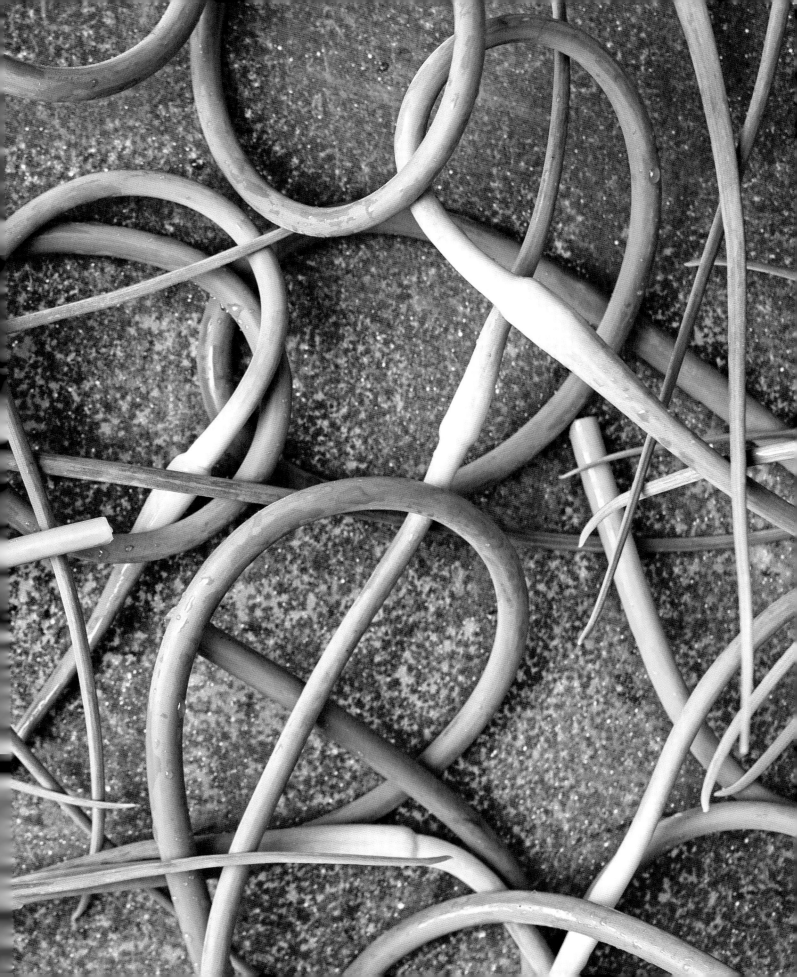

YELLOW & WHITE STORAGE ONIONS

Yellow Onions. They're our North Star. If we have yellow onions in the house, we can always find our way to dinner. And we're not alone—almost 90 percent of the storage onions grown in the US are yellow onions.

We are so accustomed to onions being available year round that we can forget that they are seasonal. Day length determines how and when onion bulbs form. In general, bulbs start growing as the summer days grow longer and warmer, although different varieties have different day length requirements. In most places, the onions' leafy green tops begin to brown and topple over sometime in late summer, the signal that the bulb below is ripe. Once the onions are harvested, they must be cured in order to make them suitable for long storage—that is, they are spread out, usually in a single layer, in a covered, dry spot with plenty of air circulation until their leaves are brittle and their necks have closed up, a process that can take a few weeks.

In the supermarket, most onions are simply labeled yellow, white or red, with the possible exception of Spanish onions—large yellow or white onions that have a milder and slightly sweeter flavor than regular yellows. However, a host of beautiful heirloom varieties, such as Ailsa Craigs and Yellow Danvers, are available to farmers and home gardeners.

ONION BIALYS MAKES 12

Bagels are a dime a dozen, but the bialy—a chewy roll with a Yiddish name whose flat center is filled with sautéed onions—is a rarer breed. The best bet is making your own. It takes some effort, but you'll be richly rewarded with handsome, oniony rolls that are primed for a shmear of cream cheese and a slice of salmon. Bialys are best eaten the day they are made, but we've had good luck freezing well-wrapped leftovers and reheating them in the oven.

FOR THE DOUGH

2¼ cups warm water

2 teaspoons active dry yeast

2 teaspoons sugar

6 to 7 cups all-purpose flour, plus more for dusting

Kosher salt

2 tablespoons butter, melted

FOR THE TOPPING

2 tablespoons butter

1 large yellow onion, finely chopped

Freshly ground black pepper

THE EVENING BEFORE YOU WANT TO BAKE the bialys, start making the sponge for the dough. Whisk together the warm water, yeast and sugar in a large bowl. Let rest for a few minutes until the mixture turns creamy. Add 2 cups flour and mix well. Cover with plastic wrap and let the sponge rise at room temperature overnight.

The next morning, make the topping. Combine the butter and onions in a small skillet and cook over moderate heat, stirring occasionally, until the onions are softened, about 5 minutes. Remove from the heat, season with several grinds of black pepper and set aside.

Return to making the dough. Stir 2 teaspoons salt into the risen sponge, then stir in enough of the remaining flour until the dough comes together in a shaggy mass. Turn the dough out onto a lightly floured work surface and knead until the dough is smooth and elastic, 8 to 10 minutes. Brush the inside of a large bowl with some of the melted butter. Shape the dough into a ball and transfer it to the bowl. Brush the top of the dough with the remaining butter, then cover the bowl tightly with plastic wrap and let rise at room temperature until doubled in size, about 1 hour.

Heat the oven to 475°F. Line 2 baking sheets with parchment. Divide the risen dough in halves and work with one half at a time, keeping the other piece covered. Cut the dough into 6 pieces and shape each into a round about 5 inches across, then press on the center to flatten. Prick the center a few times with a fork then transfer to one of the prepared baking sheets. Spoon some of the onion mixture into the center of each bialy and prick a few more times with a fork to flatten.

Put the bialys in the oven and throw a few ice cubes on the bottom of the oven. Quickly close the oven door to trap the steam and bake until the bialys are puffed, golden and browned in spots, 10 to 12 minutes. Remove from the oven and transfer to a rack to cool. While the first batch is baking, shape and fill the remaining dough. Bake the second batch as soon as the first comes out, adding more ice to the oven. Serve the bialys warm or at room temperature the same day as they are baked.

SUNDAY MORNING SALAD

MAKES ENOUGH FOR 12 BIALYS

Crisp, salty, yum. In a small bowl, combine **1 finely chopped cucumber**, **½ finely chopped small red onion**, **2 tablespoons coarsely chopped capers**, **1 teaspoon white wine vinegar** and **1 tablespoon olive oil**. Season to taste with **salt and pepper**. Split the **bialys** in half, toast lightly and spread with **cream cheese**. Top with **a few slices of smoked salmon**, a spoonful of the cucumber salad and a scattering of **chopped fresh dill**.

ALSATIAN TARTE FLAMBÉE SERVES 6 TO 8

Kate's dad ordered tarte flambée during their family's first-ever European vacation, surely on the recommendation of Rick Steves, whose book *Europe Through the Back Door* was that trip's lodestar. Dad fell in love with this creamy, onion-studded pizza (sometimes called *flammekueche*), and he made it several years running for various parties. He is not a natural cook, so it was always a treat to see him excited and having fun in the kitchen. Dad used store-bought dough and a mixture of ricotta and sour cream to replicate the flavor of crème fraîche. That combo still works in a pinch, but crème fraîche is much easier to find now than it was back in 1980s Pittsburgh. The dough can be made by hand or in a stand mixer. We waffle between the two, depending on time and how much we need a little kneading therapy. Either way doesn't take long.

FOR THE DOUGH

2 cups all-purpose flour

1 heaping teaspoon active dry yeast

Kosher salt

¾ cup warm water

2 tablespoons olive oil, plus more for oiling the bowl

FOR THE TOPPING

2 strips bacon, chopped

2 medium yellow onions, very thinly sliced

1 cup crème fraîche

Kosher salt

Freshly grated nutmeg

TO MAKE THE DOUGH, WHISK TOGETHER THE flour, yeast and ½ teaspoon salt in a large bowl (or the bowl of a stand mixer). Combine the warm water and 2 tablespoons olive oil in a measuring cup. Make a well in the center of the flour and add the water and oil. Mix together until a shaggy dough forms then turn the dough out onto a lightly floured countertop and knead until smooth (this will take 8 to 10 minutes by hand, 3 to 4 minutes in a mixer).

Drizzle some olive oil into a large bowl and use your hands to coat the sides of the bowl with oil.

Use your freshly oiled hands to gather the dough into a ball and transfer it to the bowl, rolling it all around to coat with oil. Cover the bowl with a clean kitchen towel or plastic wrap and let rise until doubled in size, 1 to 2 hours.

Meanwhile, make the topping: Cook the bacon in a small skillet over moderate heat, stirring from time to time, until softened and golden but not fully crisp, about 5 minutes. Remove from the heat.

Combine the onions and crème fraîche in a bowl. Scrape the bacon into the bowl, along with any grease from the skillet. Season the mixture with ½ teaspoon salt and a sprinkle of freshly grated nutmeg. Stir together to combine.

Heat the oven to 500°F. Lightly oil a half sheet pan, then plop the dough into the pan and stretch it to fit the pan. If it doesn't want to stretch all the way, let the dough rest for a few minutes then try again.

Spread the onion mixture evenly over the dough, going right to the edges and making sure the bacon is threaded evenly throughout. Bake until the crust is crisp and golden brown around the edges (lift up a corner of the tarte to make sure the underside is browned), about 18 minutes. Cut into squares to serve—tarte flambée is equally good hot and at room temperature.

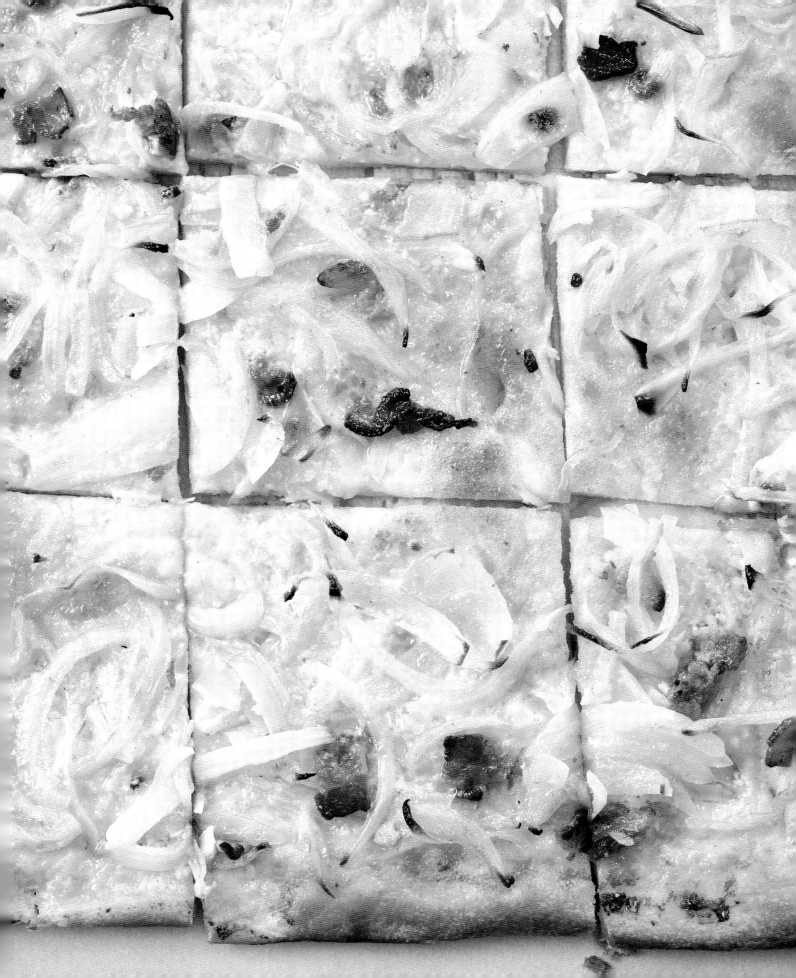

PISSALADIÈRE SERVES 8

Onions and anchovies—sweet and salty—have a real affinity for one another, and they pop up in combination time and again. In the Sicilian Sfincione (page 87), they are enriched with tomato sauce and Pecorino. In this classic French pizza, they stand alone but for a handful of briny olives. We like to serve it as an appetizer accompanied by glasses of iced rosé.

FOR THE DOUGH

2 cups all-purpose flour

1 heaping teaspoon active dry yeast

Kosher salt

¾ cup warm water

2 tablespoons olive oil, plus more for oiling the bowl and baking sheet

FOR THE TOPPING

3 pounds yellow onions, thinly sliced

6 plump garlic cloves, thinly sliced

2 sprigs fresh thyme

3 tablespoons olive oil

Kosher salt

½ cup niçoise olives

1 (2-ounce) tin oil-packed anchovies

TO MAKE THE DOUGH, COMBINE THE FLOUR, yeast and ½ teaspoon salt in the bowl of a stand mixer fitted with a dough hook. Combine the warm water and 2 tablespoons olive oil in a measuring cup. With the mixer running slowly, add the water and olive oil. Once it is fully combined, turn up the speed and knead the dough until it is smooth and pulls away from the sides of the bowl, 3 to 4 minutes. (Or remove it from the bowl and knead by hand on a lightly floured countertop for 8 to 10 minutes.) Drizzle some olive oil into a large bowl and use your hands to coat the sides of the bowl with oil.

With your oiled hands, shape the dough into a ball, then roll it all around in the bowl so it is lightly covered with oil. Cover the bowl with a clean kitchen towel or plastic wrap. Set aside to rise until doubled in size, 1 to 2 hours.

To make the topping, combine the onions, garlic, thyme, olive oil and ¼ teaspoon salt in a large heavy skillet and heat over moderate heat. Cook the mixture, stirring from time to time, until the onions are very soft, browned and caramelized, 45 to 50 minutes. After about 20 minutes of cooking, you will have to stir the softened onions more often as they begin to stick to the bottom of the pan. Scrape up that browned goodness and stir it into the onions as you go.

While the onions are cooking, pit the olives. This can be done easily by lining up several olives on a cutting board and pressing down on them with the flat side of a large knife—the pits should pop right out. Keep the olives as whole as possible.

When the onions are ready, remove them from the heat and let cool a bit. Pluck out the thyme sprigs and discard.

Heat the oven to 500°F. Generously oil a half sheet pan. Plop the dough out onto the oiled pan and, with oiled hands, stretch it out to fill the pan. If it looks like the dough is not quite making it to the edges, let it rest for a few minutes and then try again. You'll get there.

Spread the caramelized onions evenly over the dough. Dot the olives and anchovies over the dough—we like to tear the anchovies into pieces as we scatter them.

Bake the pissaladière until the crust is golden brown and crisp, about 18 minutes. Remove from the oven and serve warm or at room temperature.

GRACE'S ONION STROMBOLI SERVES 8

Our friend Grace intrigued us with tales of a recipe from her childhood in the Basilicata region of Italy in which the toppings of a pissaladière were rolled up in a thin dough made of flour, wine and olive oil. The actual recipe has been lost (it was probably never written down), but we've come to love our version based on her reminiscences.

To make it, assemble the **dough** as for Pissaladière (page 31), but replace the water with an equal amount of **white wine.** The filling remains the same, though we like to use **coarsely chopped oil-cured black olives** rather than niçoise. Roll the dough out into a large, very thin rectangle and spread end to end with the **onion mixture**. Scatter the anchovies and olives over the onions, then fold the dough in thirds, like an envelope. Place the stromboli seam-side down on a baking sheet lined with parchment and bake in a 400°F oven until deep golden brown all over, about 30 minutes. Let the stromboli cool completely before slicing.

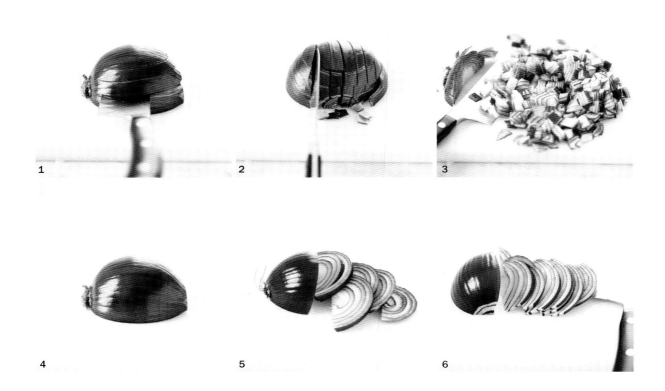

THE FIRST CUT IS THE DEEPEST

Learning how to properly chop an onion is a skill everyone should master. Most of us perform this task countless times over the course of a lifetime, and the act should provide a feeling of satisfaction, not frustration. The most important thing is to have a sharp knife. Some people swear by a large chef's knife, while others make do with a paring knife. Use whatever blade makes you most comfortable. The object is to produce neat pieces of onion that will cook evenly.

Cut the onion in half lengthwise. Peel away the skin and remove any translucent membrane covering the outermost layer, which can cause your knife to slip. Lay the onion halves cut side down on a cutting board. With your free hand holding the onion steady, make a series of horizontal slices that are parallel to the cutting board, working from the stem end and cutting almost to the root (**1**). The width between these slices is determined by how fine of a chop you want. Next, slice the onion lengthwise up to (but not through) the root (**2**). Finally, slice the onion crosswise, working from the stem toward the root (**3**). The diced pieces will fall together in a neat pile.

Many recipes in this book call for "sliced" or "thinly sliced" onions. This is what we mean: First cut the onion in half lengthwise (**4**), then cut each half crosswise into half-moons, starting at the stem end and moving in toward the root (**5**). Alternatively, cut away the root end and slice the onion lengthwise (**6**), which results in a more gently curved—dare we say, more elegant?—wedge. If onions are meant to be sliced into rings, as for fried or grilled onion rings, the recipe will state so clearly.

FRIED WATER SERVES 4

We imagine many families have a dish like this in their histories, the kind that developed during times of poverty and hunger, and that you return to in moments of nostalgia. But in this case, the food is as nourishing as the memory. Guy's mother and his great-aunt Aggie taught us how to make it, while sharing stories of Aggie's mother feeding it to them when there was nothing in the cupboard but onions, eggs and a heel of bread.

The general formula to remember is 1 onion + 1 egg + 1¼ cups water per person, so it's as easy to make for a family of 8 as for just one. If you're feeling flush, shower a little freshly grated Parmigiano over the dish.

4 medium yellow onions, sliced

⅓ cup olive oil

5 cups water

4 large eggs

Kosher salt and freshly ground black pepper

4 thick slices stale bread

COMBINE THE ONIONS AND OLIVE OIL IN A large skillet and cook gently over moderate heat ("low and slow," as Aggie says) until the onions are softened and shiny but have not taken on any color, about 10 minutes. Add the water and bring to a boil, then reduce the heat to moderately low and simmer until the onions are soft, silky and can "melt in your mouth," about 10 minutes.

Meanwhile, beat the eggs with 1 teaspoon kosher salt. Turn off the heat under the onions and slowly drizzle in the eggs, stirring all the while with a fork—the eggs will cook into soft threads. Season the mixture with salt and pepper to taste.

To serve, set out 4 shallow soup bowls and lay a slice of stale bread in each. Ladle the fried water over the bread and serve at once.

CHICKEN AND EGG SOUP SERVES 1

When you tell people you're writing a cookbook about alliums, everyone immediately shares their favorite recipe. This is one we learned of in our local coffee shop, promptly played around with and made our own. It's the kind of dish you make for yourself to eat in happy solitude. The flavors will go in completely different directions depending on whether you use the verdurette (classic soup flavorings) or vadouvan (more Indian-inflected), but either way, use the best chicken broth you can.

Chop **1 yellow onion** and put it in a small pot with **1 tablespoon olive oil**. Cook over moderate heat, stirring from time to time, until softened and golden, about 15 minutes. While the onions cook, finely chop **1 plum tomato**. Stir the tomato and **1 heaping tablespoon Vadouvan** (page 117) or **Christine's Verdurette** (page 228) into the onions and cook until softened and fragrant, about 2 minutes. Add **2 cups chicken broth** and bring to a simmer. Season to taste with **kosher salt and freshly ground black pepper**. Crack **1 large egg** into the center of the simmering soup and poach for 2 minutes. Transfer the soup to a warm bowl and stir well to break up the egg. Eat at once.

FRENCH ONION SOUP SERVES 6

This may be the gateway dish to allium addiction. As a child, you come for the cheese, but as an adult, you stay for the velvety onions. Some French onion soups are so cheesy that you spend the entire meal pulling scalding hot strands from your lips and shirtfront. This version with scallions and a garnish of chives is a little more refined, and there's no need to maneuver sloshing bowls of hot soup in and out of the broiler.

3 pounds yellow onions, thinly sliced

1 large thyme sprig

1 bay leaf

2 tablespoons olive oil, plus more for brushing the bread

1 cup grated Gruyère

¼ cup freshly grated Parmesan

3 scallions, thinly sliced

4 large slices country bread

8 cups Beef Stock (page 37)

Kosher salt and freshly ground black pepper

½ cup dry vermouth

Chopped chives, for garnish

COMBINE THE ONIONS, THYME, BAY LEAF AND olive oil in a heavy pot over moderate heat and cook gently until the onions are softened and deep golden brown, 30 to 40 minutes. Stir the onions often, especially as you reach the end of the cooking time, to make sure they don't scorch.

While the onions cook, gently combine the Gruyère, Parmesan and scallions in a bowl. Cut the slices of bread into smaller pieces—quarters or long fingers—so that they will fit well in your soup bowls. Arrange the bread on a baking sheet and brush lightly with olive oil.

Heat the stock over low heat and keep warm, covered. When the onions are fully cooked, pluck out the bay leaf and thyme sprig and season the onions with 1 teaspoon salt and several grinds of black pepper. Add the warm broth and the vermouth and simmer for about 10 minutes. Taste and adjust the seasonings as needed. Keep warm over low heat.

Heat the oven to 450°F. Toast the bread in the oven until golden brown and crisp. Remove the toasts from the oven and turn on the broiler. Top each toast with a heap of the grated cheese mixture. Broil the toasts until the cheese has melted to a delicious golden brown. Ladle the soup into warm bowls and float a couple of cheesy toasts on top of each serving. Sprinkle some chives over each bowl and serve at once.

SOME LIKE IT COLD

Many recipes call for heating oil in a skillet before adding onions, but we picked up the habit of combining onions and oil in a cold skillet and heating them up together from cooking instructor Fabrizia Lanza. It's often a matter of convenience to chop the onions first and dump them in a skillet to get them out of the way while you prep the remaining ingredients of a recipe, but like Fabrizia, we have come to appreciate how evenly onions cook when they heat up at the same rate as the oil.

BEEF STOCK MAKES ABOUT 8 CUPS

French onion soup is only as good as the stock with which it is made. An aseptic container of organic stock may be cheaper and easier, but it will never be as delicious. Plus, you can shred the long-cooked short rib meat after it's flavored the stock, and repurpose it in *Beef Empanadas with Raisins and Olives* (page 40). Make this the day before you plan to use it; it's much easier to remove the fat once the stock has chilled.

2 large yellow onions

2 carrots

1 celery rib

5 pounds meaty beef short ribs

Kosher salt and freshly ground black pepper

16 cups water

3 sprigs fresh parsley

2 sprigs fresh thyme

1 bay leaf

HEAT THE OVEN TO 450°F. QUARTER THE unpeeled onions and cut the carrots and celery into large chunks. Place the vegetables in a large roasting pan. Season the short ribs all over with salt and pepper and add to the pan. Roast in the oven, turning once, until everything is well browned, about 1 hour.

Scrape the short ribs and vegetables into a large stockpot, then place the roasting pan on the stovetop over moderately high heat. Add 2 cups water and bring to a boil. Deglaze the pan by stirring and scraping the browned bits left in the bottom, then add it all to the pot.

Add the parsley, thyme, bay leaf and remaining 14 cups water to the pot and bring to a boil over high heat. Reduce the heat to moderately low and cook, uncovered, at a very gentle simmer until the stock has reduced to about 8 cups, which should take about 4 hours. Skim off the foam that rises to the top as the stock simmers.

If you want to save the cooked meat for empanadas or another dish, use tongs to pluck the ribs from the stock and place on a platter to cool. Strain the stock through a fine-mesh sieve, discarding the vegetables and herbs, and let it cool completely at room temperature before refrigerating overnight.

The following day remove the layer of fat from the stock, then use the stock to make French Onion Soup (page 36) or transfer to smaller airtight containers and freeze for up to 6 months.

BEEF EMPANADAS WITH RAISINS AND OLIVES MAKES ABOUT 45 EMPANADAS

It can be downright painful to throw out $50 worth of short ribs after making Beef Stock (page 37). True, only a whisper of flavor clings to the beef after it has simmered away for hours, but pairing it with deep spices, raisins and olives gives it a second life. Having a stash of these flaky empanadas in the freezer will make you feel like a superhero when unexpected guests show up. Make them once and you'll want to make them again. To do so without the benefit of leftover short ribs, substitute about 1½ pounds ground beef, adding it in place of the shredded beef, but taking the time to cook it through. The dough is a breeze to work with, but we won't snitch if you substitute frozen empanada discs.

FOR THE DOUGH

½ cup butter

¼ cup vegetable shortening or lard

Kosher salt

2 cups boiling water

6 cups all-purpose flour, or as needed

FOR THE FILLING

2 medium yellow or white onions, finely chopped

2 tablespoons olive oil

1 teaspoon ancho chile powder

1 teaspoon ground cumin

½ teaspoon smoked paprika

1 Yukon Gold potato, finely chopped

1½ cups water

Kosher salt and freshly ground black pepper

5 pounds cooked beef short ribs, left over from making Beef Stock (page 37)

½ cup green olives, pitted and coarsely chopped

¼ cup raisins or currants

1 large egg, lightly beaten

TO MAKE THE DOUGH, CUT THE BUTTER INTO pieces and place in a large bowl. Add the shortening and 1 teaspoon salt. Pour the boiling water over the butter and shortening and stir together until they are melted. Let cool for a few minutes, then add the flour and stir until a rough dough comes together. Transfer to a floured surface and knead until smooth, about 5 minutes, adding more flour if the dough is very sticky. Shape the dough into a ball, wrap it in plastic wrap and refrigerate it for at least 1 hour and up to 3 hours.

While the dough rests, make the filling. Combine the onions and olive oil in a skillet over moderately high heat and cook, stirring from time to time, until softened, about 10 minutes. Add the chile powder, cumin and paprika and cook, stirring, until very fragrant, about 1 minute. Add the potato and stir to coat with the spices, then stir in 1 cup water and season with ½ teaspoon salt and several grinds of black pepper. Reduce the heat to moderately low and simmer gently.

While the mixture simmers, finely shred the beef with your fingers, discarding bones and large bits of fat. Stir the beef into the simmering mixture and cook until warmed through, adding the remaining ½ cup water to loosen it. Season with salt to taste. Stir in the olives and raisins and simmer for 5 minutes more. Remove from the heat; taste and adjust the seasonings. Let cool.

Heat the oven to 425°F. Line a baking sheet with parchment. Cut the dough in half and roll it out on a lightly floured surface until it is about ⅛ inch thick. Using a 3½-inch round cookie cutter, cut as many rounds from the dough as you can. Gather up the scraps into a ball and wrap in plastic wrap. Roll out each circle individually to make them a little thinner. Place about 1 tablespoon filling in the center of each dough round. Brush the edges with some beaten egg and fold over to seal, crimping the edges by hand or with the tines of a fork. Transfer the finished empanadas to the baking sheet as you work. Continue with the remaining dough and filling, rerolling the dough scraps once.

Brush the tops of the empanadas with the remaining egg wash. Bake the empanadas until the pastry is golden brown, 20 to 25 minutes. Remove from the oven and serve warm.

NOTE: The empanadas can be shaped and frozen in a single layer on a parchment-lined baking sheet. Once frozen, transfer to a resealable plastic bag and freeze for up to 3 months. Brush the frozen empanadas with egg wash and bake at 425°F until golden brown and piping hot, about 25 minutes.

FIGHTING TEARS

A cook's biggest complaint about chopping onions is the fear of tears. Cutting an onion begins a chain reaction, as organic sulfur compounds are formed and enzymes are released that can cause our eyes to water and noses to run. Many times, chopping onions has no effect at all while other times we've stood at the cutting board sobbing our hearts out. Grabbing an onion can feel like a game of roulette.

Both cold and water render the enzyme-produced chemical less volatile, hence many cooks suggest chilling onions for thirty minutes or so before chopping them, or chopping the onions under running water, though for the life of us we've never figured out how to do that! We've met some success with a method that combines the two ideas—placing halved onions in a dish of cold water before cutting them.

Over the years, Kate has determined that wearing her contact lenses offers a measure of protection that regular eyeglasses do not. And we have found that, not surprisingly, a sharp knife is better than a dull one, if only to get through the task more quickly and neatly. And really, like so much of life, there's no way through it but to do it. After chopping a particularly brutal onion, we rub our hands with half of a lemon before washing them with soap and water, a ritual that seems to stem the tide of tears.

CURRIED ONION FRITTERS WITH MINT RAITA MAKES ABOUT 16 FRITTERS

Similar to the spicy Indian snack, onion bhaji, these fritters should be tongue-numbingly hot, so that you crave the cool relief of the raita. Make them to slake your hunger while a curry bubbles away on the back of the stove, and eat them as they are fried, preferably with a cold beer in hand.

FOR THE RAITA

1 cup plain whole-milk yogurt

2 small cucumbers, such as Persian, finely chopped

1 tablespoon finely chopped mint

Kosher salt and freshly ground black pepper

FOR THE FRITTERS

3 medium yellow onions, thinly sliced

2 serrano chiles, thinly sliced

3 tablespoons chopped cilantro

1 tablespoon curry powder

½ teaspoon cayenne

Kosher salt and freshly ground black pepper

½ cup chickpea flour

1 large egg, lightly beaten

Peanut or vegetable oil, for frying

TO MAKE THE RAITA, COMBINE THE YOGURT, cucumbers and mint in a small bowl. Season with ¼ teaspoon salt and several grinds of black pepper. Refrigerate until ready to serve.

To make the fritters, combine the onions, chiles and cilantro in a large bowl. Add the curry powder, cayenne, 1 teaspoon salt and several grinds of black pepper and toss everything together until well combined. Sprinkle the chickpea flour over the onion mixture, add the egg and mix together gently so everything is lightly coated.

Heat about ½ inch oil in a heavy skillet over moderately high heat. While the oil heats up, lay some paper towels on a cooling rack or a platter. When the oil is hot and shimmering, use two forks to scoop up about 2 tablespoons of the onion mixture. Drop the mixture into the oil, pressing down lightly so it spreads out a bit. Some of the onions will straggle out, which is totally fine—these bits will become extra crunchy. Fry the fritters until deep golden brown on the underside, 2 to 3 minutes, then flip and continue to fry about 2 minutes more. Transfer the fritters to the paper towels to drain, and scoop out any floating bits from the oil before frying another batch. Eat the fritters while they are hot, dabbed with a spoonful of raita.

HANUKKAH TREE-TRIMMING LATKES MAKES ABOUT 18 LATKES

One of our dearest holiday traditions is a mashup we've come to call Hanukkah Tree-Trimming. We squash into our friends' John and Nancy's Brooklyn apartment, make Christmas ornaments, decorate their tree and feast on John's perfect latkes. The ratio you need to know is two potatoes to one onion. From there, you can scale up as needed, and when making latkes, you should always scale up—running out is not an option! For most, they're a once-a-year treat, so we say it's okay to eat as many as humanly possible that day.

4 large russet potatoes, peeled

2 medium yellow onions, quartered

Kosher salt and freshly ground black pepper

2 large eggs

Peanut or vegetable oil, for frying

Applesauce and sour cream, for serving

INSERT YOUR FOOD PROCESSOR'S SHRED-ding blade. If possible, remove the smaller feed tube at the top of the food processor, so that the potatoes can lie in the tube horizontally, which will give you maximum potato strand length.

Grate the potatoes, laying them horizontally in the feed tube. Grate the onions on top of the potatoes; their juices will help keep the potatoes from turning brown. Transfer the potatoes and onions to a large bowl and toss with 2 teaspoons salt and several grinds of black pepper. Crack the eggs into the bowl and stir well to combine. Transfer the mixture to a large colander and set the colander inside the bowl. The potato mixture will give off lots of liquid, which you want to squeeze out to make the crispest latkes possible; the colander helps the draining process.

Pour about ⅛ inch oil into a large cast-iron or other heavy skillet and heat over moderately high heat. While the oil heats up, lay some newspapers, clean paper bags or paper towels on a cooling rack. When the oil is hot enough (a shred of potato will sizzle immediately in it when ready), scoop up about ¼ cup of the potato mixture and give it a good squeeze to rid it of most of its moisture. Shape the mixture into a thin patty, about 3 inches wide, and slip it into the oil, flattening it a bit with a spatula. Don't worry if some shreds of potatoes straggle out—they will provide extra crunch. Make as many latkes as will fit comfortably in the skillet without crowding them and fry until deep golden brown, about 5 minutes per side. Transfer the latkes to the lined rack and sprinkle with salt. Make sure to scoop out any bits of potato or onion that break away from a latke so they don't burn and make the oil bitter. Add a bit more oil if it begins to get low, letting it come up to tempera-ture before you add more latkes.

It's best to eat the latkes as you make them, set out with bowls of applesauce and sour cream for people to add as they like. But a leftover latke is better than no latke at all, and you can reheat them, set on a cooling rack, in a 350°F oven until heated through and crisp, about 8 minutes.

SUMMER SAUCE
MAKES ENOUGH
FOR 1 POUND PASTA

We make this sauce in the sultry, steamy days of August, when we crave pasta but only want to heat up the kitchen long enough to cook the noodles (tip: start with hot water, cover the pot while it comes to a boil and cook it fast!). Grating is an easy way to get rid of the tomato skins, but if you don't care so much, you can also just chop the tomatoes and onions. If we are lucky enough to have some leftover Basil Pesto (page 306) in the fridge, we'll add dollops of it to our plates. Ditto for grilled vegetables. Grated ricotta salata or big cubes of juicy mozzarella are always welcome, too.

Cut **2 pounds ripe tomatoes** in half then grate them over the large holes of a box grater, directly into a large bowl; you will be left with just the skins. Peel **1 small red onion** and grate it over the tomatoes. Stir in **⅓ cup good olive oil**, **1 tablespoon sherry vinegar** and **1 teaspoon kosher salt**. Let the mixture marinate for an hour or so before stirring in the hot pasta.

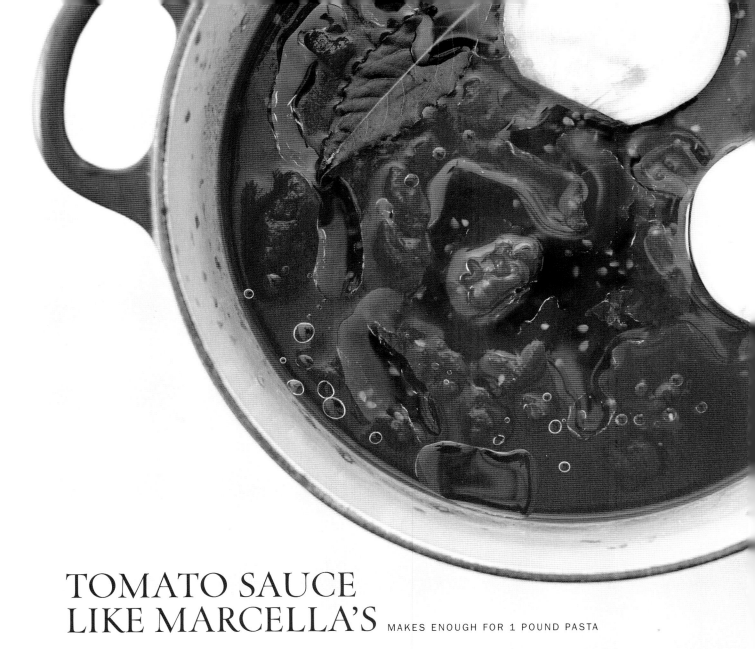

TOMATO SAUCE LIKE MARCELLA'S

MAKES ENOUGH FOR 1 POUND PASTA

When we're too weary to even chop an onion, it's time to make Marcella Hazan's famous sauce. Over the years, it has averted many hungry tears and happily fed many last-minute guests. Her recipe traditionally calls for butter, but we prefer the lighter flavor that comes from using olive oil. Some nights we like to add a pinch of good dried oregano or a bit of crushed red pepper flakes. Memorize this recipe once and it will feed you forever.

Open **1 (28-ounce) can plum tomatoes in juice**. Holding a tomato over a medium saucepan, use a small paring knife to shear off the hard stem end; discard it. Squeeze the tomato in your hand to crush it and drop into the saucepan (work inside the saucepan to keep the juice from splattering everywhere). Continue with the remaining tomatoes, then add the juice from the can to the pot. Peel **1 medium yellow or red onion**, trim the root end and halve it lengthwise. Add the onion halves to the pan, along with **1 bay leaf, ¼ cup good olive oil** and **½ teaspoon kosher salt**. Bring the mixture to a simmer over moderate heat and simmer away for 20 to 25 minutes, giving a stir from time to time. This is enough time for the flavors to come together while staying fresh and light (much longer and the sauce will become too concentrated and sludgy). It's also just the right amount of time to get a pot of water on to boil, make a salad dressing and wash your greens.

AUNT EMMA'S PIEROGI MAKES ABOUT 2 DOZEN LARGE PIEROGI

One of Kate's earliest memories is of walking into her great-great aunt's home and being greeted by the scent of onions sizzling in butter—one of the sweetest smells in the world. Aunt Emma, a Polish immigrant who lived in the Morningside neighborhood of Pittsburgh, seemed ancient and birdlike—a little wren in cat's-eye glasses—but boy, could she cook. Her pound cake was dense and moist, her fried *chrusciki* could float away and her pierogi were magnificent, the gold standard against which all other pierogi have been measured. They were generous and pillowy, slicked with butter and lapped by soft, translucent onions. We can only hope that ours would make her proud. When we make a batch, we usually cook some right away and freeze the rest to enjoy later.

FOR THE PIEROGI

4 cups all-purpose flour

Kosher salt

½ cup whole milk

½ cup water

1 large egg

2 tablespoons sour cream

2 large russet potatoes

4 tablespoons butter, cut into pieces

1½ cups farmers cheese

Freshly ground black pepper

FOR COOKING EVERY 6 PIEROGI

6 tablespoons butter

1 yellow onion, thinly sliced

TO MAKE THE PIEROGI, WHISK TOGETHER THE flour and ½ teaspoon salt in a large bowl. Combine the milk and water in a large glass measuring cup. Crack the egg into it and add the sour cream, whisking everything together. Add the liquid ingredients to the flour and stir until a soft dough forms. Dust your counter and hands with flour and turn the dough out. Knead the dough, adding a little more flour as needed, until it is smooth and no longer sticky, about 10 minutes. Go easy on adding flour—too much will make the dough tough—and trust that it will come together with time. Shape the dough into a ball and cover with plastic wrap. Set aside at room temperature while you make the filling.

Peel the potatoes and cut them into chunks. Put the potatoes and 2 teaspoons salt into a saucepan and cover with cold water. Bring to a boil then reduce the heat to moderate and simmer until the potatoes are very tender, 15 to 20 minutes. Drain well and transfer to a bowl. Add the butter and farmers cheese to the warm potatoes and mash everything together until very smooth. Season the mixture with salt and pepper to taste. Set aside to cool completely.

Line two baking sheets with parchment and sprinkle lightly with flour. Sprinkle some flour on the counter. Set out a small bowl of water, along with a fork for sealing the pierogi.

Using a sharp knife, cut off about a third of the dough, keeping the rest wrapped in plastic. Sprinkle the dough lightly with flour then roll it out very thin, about 1/16 inch thick. If the dough resists stretching, let it rest for a few minutes. Using a 5-inch round cookie cutter or a sharp paring knife with a small bowl as a guide, cut the dough into circles. Gather the scraps together, press into a ball and wrap in plastic, rerolling the scraps once.

Scoop about 2 tablespoons of the cooled filling onto the center of each dough round. Dip a finger into the bowl of water and moisten the edge of a dough round. Fold the dough over to make a half moon then seal by pressing the tines of the fork around the edge of the dough. Repeat with the remaining dough rounds, transferring the finished pierogi to the baking sheet as you go, making sure they don't touch and stick together.

If you plan on cooking the pierogi right away, bring a large pot of water to a boil. (To freeze the pierogi for later, set the baking sheets in the freezer until the pierogi are frozen through, about 1 hour, then transfer the pierogi to resealable plastic bags and store in the freezer. Frozen pierogies can be added directly to boiling water.)

About 6 pierogi will fit into a large cast-iron skillet at a time. Melt 6 tablespoons butter in the skillet over moderate heat. Add the sliced onions and cook gently, stirring from time to time, until the onions are tender but not browned, 10 to 12 minutes. Keep warm over low heat while you boil the pierogi.

Salt the boiling water and slip 6 pierogi at a time into the water. They will sink (stir them gently so they don't stick to the bottom of the pot) and then rise again. Once the pierogi come to the surface, cook them until the dough is tender, 3 to 4 minutes. Use a slotted spoon to drain the pierogi then transfer to the skillet. Increase the heat to moderate and cook the pierogi until they are lightly browned in spots, flipping once, 8 to 10 minutes. Keep cooked pierogi warm as you cook the rest, adding more butter and onions for each batch.

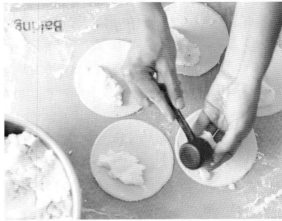

HROUS-SPICED CHICKEN MEATBALLS WITH COUSCOUS SERVES 4 TO 6

Once you have the spice paste made, these North African–inspired meatballs rely on pantry staples and come together quickly on a weeknight. When making meatballs, we almost always use ground chicken or turkey since the lean meat is enriched by plenty of bread crumbs, egg and herbs.

1 cup bread crumbs

⅓ cup whole milk

1 pound ground chicken or turkey, preferably thigh meat

¼ cup plus 1 tablespoon Hrous (page 56)

1 bunch scallions, finely chopped

2 tablespoons finely chopped mint

2 tablespoons finely chopped parsley

2 tablespoons finely chopped cilantro

1 large egg, lightly beaten

Kosher salt and freshly ground black pepper

¼ cup olive oil

1 yellow or red onion, finely chopped

1 (28-ounce) can diced tomatoes

½ cup golden raisins

1 teaspoon red wine vinegar

Steamed couscous, for serving

COMBINE THE BREAD CRUMBS AND MILK IN a small bowl to soak. Line a baking sheet or a tray with a piece of parchment paper.

Combine the ground chicken, ¼ cup hrous, scallions, mint, parsley and cilantro in a bowl. Squeeze any excess moisture from the bread crumbs then add the crumbs to the chicken mixture, along with the egg, ½ teaspoon salt and several grinds of black pepper. Using your hands, mix everything together gently but thoroughly. Shape the chicken mixture into 2-inch balls—you should be able to make 18 to 20 meatballs.

Heat the olive oil in a large heavy skillet over moderately high heat. Add the meatballs and cook, turning occasionally, until browned all over, 8 to 10 minutes.

Once the meatballs are browned, transfer them to a platter. Add the onions to the skillet, reduce the heat to moderate and cook, stirring from time to time, until the onions are softened, about 5 minutes. Add the remaining 1 tablespoon hrous and cook, stirring, for 1 minute. Add the tomatoes with their juice and bring to a simmer. Simmer over moderately low heat for 10 minutes, then add the raisins and ½ teaspoon salt and simmer for another 10 minutes.

Add the meatballs back to the sauce and simmer until the meatballs are cooked through, about 12 minutes. Stir in the vinegar, taste and adjust the seasonings. Serve the meatballs and sauce over steamed couscous.

HROUS
TUNISIAN ONION-CHILE PASTE MAKES ABOUT 2 CUPS

So much of our knowledge of Mediterranean, Middle Eastern and North African cooking comes from the pages of Paula Wolfert's books. Hrous—a spectacular combination of lightly fermented onions, dried chiles and spices—is one of our favorite finds. We call for it in a number of recipes in this book, and it could be happily smeared on almost anything before it hits the grill—steaks, vegetables, fish, you name it. It is easy to make but requires patience—you must wait at least one month before digging in, but the longer the hrous sits, the better. Over time, it becomes mellower, richer, deeper.

2 large yellow onions, thinly sliced

½ teaspoon ground turmeric

Kosher salt

3 ounces dried New Mexico red chiles, stemmed and seeded

1½ teaspoons caraway seeds

1 teaspoon coriander seeds

½ teaspoon cumin seeds

½ teaspoon black peppercorns

¼ teaspoon ground cinnamon

⅓ cup extra-virgin olive oil

COMBINE THE ONIONS, TURMERIC AND 3 tablespoons salt in a bowl. Cover with a clean kitchen towel and let stand at room temperature for 3 days.

At the end of the fermenting time, drain the onions in a sieve, pressing on them to extract some of the moisture. Transfer the onions to a food processor, along with the chiles.

Combine the caraway, coriander, cumin and peppercorns in a small skillet and toast over moderately low heat, stirring to keep the spices from burning, until fragrant, about 2 minutes. Remove from the heat and transfer to the processor, along with the cinnamon. Process until everything is finely ground and combined. Transfer to a pint jar, packing down to prevent any air pockets. Pour the oil over the mixture to cover, seal and refrigerate for at least 1 month before using. The mixture will keep, refrigerated, up to a year.

BRAISED LAMB SHANKS WITH CHERMOULA SERVES 4

Like Hrous-Spiced Chicken Meatballs with Couscous (page 55), these lamb shanks are tinged with North African flavors, from the spice paste marinade for the lamb to the bright, herby chermoula that finishes the dish. We like to serve the shanks over steamed rice or roasted eggplant. There's plenty of time to make a batch of Scallion Nigella Flatbreads (page 154) while the lamb bubbles away—they're perfect for mopping up the sauce.

4 lamb shanks (2 to 3 pounds total)

Kosher salt and freshly ground black pepper

¼ cup Hrous (page 56)

3 tablespoons olive oil

1 yellow onion, finely chopped

1 carrot, finely chopped

1 celery rib, finely chopped

2 plump garlic cloves, finely chopped

1 tablespoon tomato paste

1 cinnamon stick

4 cups chicken broth

Chermoula (page 303), for serving

SEASON THE LAMB SHANKS THOROUGHLY with salt and pepper, then rub the hrous paste all over the shanks. Cover tightly and marinate overnight in the refrigerator.

Heat the olive oil in a medium Dutch oven or heavy pot over moderately high heat. Add the lamb shanks and brown on all sides, 8 to 10 minutes. Transfer the shanks to a platter and add the onions, carrots, celery and garlic to the pot. Cook the vegetables, stirring and scraping up the browned bits on the bottom, until golden and softened, about 8 minutes. Season with salt and pepper then scoot the vegetables over to the side of the pot and add the tomato paste and the cinnamon stick. Cook, stirring all the while, until the paste is a shade darker, about 2 minutes. Stir the paste into the vegetables, then add the chicken broth and bring to a simmer.

Return the shanks to the pot, along with any juices or remaining bits of marinade that have collected on the platter. Reduce the heat to moderately low and simmer, covered, until the shanks are very tender, about 2 hours.

Uncover the pot and let the sauce bubble away for a few minutes until slightly reduced and thickened. Skim off some fat from the top of the sauce.

To serve, divide the shanks and sauce among shallow bowls. Top each shank with a generous spoonful of chermoula.

NOTE: The lamb shanks can be made a day or two in advance. Let them cool completely in the sauce, uncovered, then cover and refrigerate until cold. Remove any solidified fat from the surface of the sauce before gently reheating the shanks.

RED BEANS AND RICE
SERVES 6 (OR 1 COUPLE FOR ALMOST AN ENTIRE WEEK)

A lifetime ago for Kate's birthday, we asked friends and family to share their favorite recipe as a gift. It was so interesting to see what people chose (and to see how many people couldn't settle on just one recipe!)—most seemed to gravitate toward the kind of dish that you could be perfectly content eating every day for the rest of your life. Cookbook author Cheryl Jamison shared her recipe for Cajun-style red beans and rice, and it is just that kind of dish: nourishing, complete—a keeper. We have made it many times over the years, and Cheryl's steady comfort has become ours as well.

1 pound dried red beans

2 medium yellow onions, chopped

2 celery ribs, chopped

1 green bell pepper, cored and chopped

4 plump garlic cloves, finely chopped

1 to 2 smoked ham hocks

2 bay leaves

½ to 1 teaspoon cayenne pepper

Kosher salt and freshly ground black pepper

Steamed white rice, for serving

Sliced scallions and Louisiana hot pepper sauce, for serving

THE NIGHT BEFORE YOU PLAN TO COOK THE beans, put them in a large heavy pot and cover with cold water by 4 inches. Set the beans aside to soak overnight.

The next day, add the onions, celery, bell pepper, garlic, ham hocks and bay leaves to the beans. Stir in the cayenne, 1 tablespoon salt and lots of freshly ground black pepper.

Set the pot on the stove and bring to a boil over high heat. Reduce the heat to low and cook the beans, uncovered, at a very gentle simmer, stirring often, until extremely tender and beginning to break apart, about 2 hours. Add more hot water whenever the beans begin to get dry; the cooking liquid should become thick and creamy, almost gravy-like. Remove the ham hocks and discard (the meat will have transported all its flavor to the beans by this point). Taste the beans and adjust the seasonings as needed. Like so many slow-cooked dishes, the beans will taste even better if you make them far enough in advance to cool, refrigerate and later reheat.

To serve, spoon the steamed rice into shallow bowls, then top each with a generous ladle of beans. Serve piping hot, with scallions and hot sauce on the side for everyone to add as they like.

KOSHARY

SERVES 2 TO 3, BUT EASILY INCREASED AS NEEDED

There's nothing fancy about koshary—indeed, one could argue that it's a great way to clean out the fridge—but this classic Egyptian dish of lentils, rice and pasta couldn't be tastier or more satisfying. We speak from experience when we say that small children love it, and it makes a fine antidote to a hangover. Don't skip the last-minute swirl of minty butter, which makes this bowl of earthy flavors take flight.

1 cup-ish leftover cooked pasta or ½ cup uncooked ditalini or macaroni

1 large yellow onion, coarsely chopped

2 tablespoons olive oil

1 cup-ish leftover tomato sauce

1 cup-ish cooked lentils (or leftover Lentil Salad 101, page 96)

1 cup-ish cooked white or brown rice

Kosher salt and freshly ground black pepper

2 tablespoons butter

2 tablespoons chopped mint

Pinch of crushed red pepper flakes

IF YOU DON'T HAVE LEFTOVER PASTA ON hand, bring a small pot of salted water to a boil and cook the ditalini until al dente. Drain.

Heat the onions and olive oil in a medium skillet over moderately high heat and cook, stirring from time to time, until the onions are golden and browned in spots, 10 to 12 minutes. Add the tomato sauce and bring to a simmer. Stir in the lentils and rice and cook until heated through. Add the pasta and cook until heated through, a matter of a few minutes. Season to taste with salt and pepper. Transfer the mixture to bowls and keep warm on the stove while you make the buttery mint sauce.

Heat the butter in a small skillet over moderately high heat. When it foams, toss in the mint leaves and a pinch of crushed red pepper flakes—they will sizzle and spit—and swirl the pan to combine. Remove from the heat and immediately pour the seasoned butter over the bowls of koshary. Serve at once.

SAVE YOUR SKINS

When making something that calls for a lot of onions, like Sunday Brisket with Onions (page 67) or Caramelized Onions (page 121), the skins can really pile up. Of course, you can just throw them in the compost bin, but if you're feeling a little more creative, you can boil the skins in water with a few drops of vinegar and dye eggs with them. The colors will be subtle but very pretty. (Friends who like to keep hard-boiled eggs in the fridge as a ready snack will often boil the eggs with onion skins so they can tell at a glance which eggs are raw and which are cooked.) Onion skins can also be used for dying wool or fabric, as well as hair. Drinking hot tea made from onion skins is said to help a cough. We always include the onion skins when making chicken or vegetable stock—it helps enrich the color and deepen the flavor.

MUSTARD-CRUMBED PORK CHOPS WITH APPLES AND ONIONS SERVES 4 TO 6

As a child, Kate read the *Little House on the Prairie* books over and over. They are full of fantastic descriptions of food, but perhaps none so much as *Farmer Boy*, Laura Ingalls Wilder's tale of her husband's childhood in upstate New York. She writes of how much Almanzo loved fried apples 'n' onions: When "…they went in to dinner, there on the table was a big dish of them! Mother knew what he liked best, and she had cooked it for him." We remembered that passage one recent autumn, when our neighbor's two overgrown apple trees surprised us with a bumper crop. The apples looked gnarly but tasted wonderful, with crisp, tart flesh. Like an apple picking bucket brigade, our family crossed the street again and again to load up our baskets before the deer ate them all. After we had our fill of applesauce, we made a big skillet of fried apples and onions, and enjoyed them just as much as Almanzo did.

1½ pounds boneless pork chops

Kosher salt and freshly ground black pepper

⅓ cup Dijon mustard

1 cup fresh breadcrumbs

4 tablespoons butter

4 tablespoons olive oil

6 small unpeeled apples, thinly sliced

2 large yellow onions, thinly sliced

USING A MEAT POUNDER OR THE SIDE OF A rolling pin, pound the pork chops between sheets of plastic wrap until they are an even ¼ inch thick. Season them all over with salt and pepper. Spread a thin layer of mustard on both sides of the chops, then dredge lightly in the breadcrumbs to coat. Set aside on parchment while you prepare the apples and onions.

Heat 2 tablespoons butter and 2 tablespoons olive oil in a large heavy skillet over moderately high heat. Add the apples and onions, cover and cook for about 2 minutes until they begin to soften. Uncover the skillet, season with salt and pepper and continue to cook, stirring gently from time to time, until the apples and onions are softened but still have some bite, 8 to 10 minutes more. Transfer to a platter and cover loosely to keep warm.

Wipe out the skillet, add the remaining 2 tablespoons butter and 2 tablespoons olive oil and heat over moderately high heat. Depending on the size of the skillet, you may have to cook the chops in batches or use 2 pans. When the butter foams, add the breaded chops and cook until golden brown and crisp on one side, about 3 minutes. Flip carefully and cook until the bottom crumbs are golden brown and the pork is cooked through and juicy, another 2 to 3 minutes. Remove from the heat and serve right away with the warm apples and onions.

SUNDAY BRISKET WITH ONIONS SERVES 6

Juicy brisket cooked in a sauce of meltingly tender onions epitomizes Sunday night fare—comforting, uncomplicated and able to feed a big family. But, like all braises, it only improves if made ahead. So cook it on Sunday afternoon and look forward to a ready-made meal later in the week.

1 (4-pound) beef brisket

Kosher salt and freshly ground black pepper

2 tablespoons olive oil

3 pounds yellow onions, thinly sliced

1 bay leaf

1 tablespoon apple cider vinegar

1 tablespoon Dijon mustard

1 (12-ounce) bottle or can of beer

HEAT THE OVEN TO 350°F. TRIM THE EXCESS fat from the brisket (keep some on for flavor and juiciness) and season well with salt and pepper. Heat the olive oil in a large Dutch oven or heavy pot over moderately high heat, then add the brisket and sear, turning once, until browned on both sides, 8 to 10 minutes. Transfer the brisket to a platter.

Add the onions, bay leaf and ½ teaspoon salt to the pot. Cook, stirring and scraping, until they have softened, about 10 minutes.

Stir the vinegar and mustard into the onions, then pull out about half the onions. Return the brisket to the pot, nestling it into the onions and top with the reserved onions. Pour in the beer, cover tightly and transfer to the oven. Braise until the beef is very tender, 3 to 3½ hours.

Remove from the oven, uncover and let the meat and sauce cool completely. Cover and refrigerate overnight or up to 3 days.

Before serving, lift out and discard the fat that has solidified on the surface of the sauce. Discard the bay leaf. Remove the brisket and slice it thinly against the grain. Nestle the meat back into the sauce and reheat gently in a low oven.

If you must serve the brisket the day you braise it, let it cool about 30 minutes. Then skim off some of the fat from the sauce, slice the brisket against the grain and serve.

TUESDAY'S SHEPHERD'S PIE
SERVES A FAMILY OF 3 OR 4 VERY HAPPILY

Our son's favorite part of the brisket is the leftovers, which we turn into shepherd's pie. We coarsely chop the leftover meat and glistening onions and then figure the quantities needed to round out the meal. For about **2 cups meat and onions,** peel **2 large or 6 to 8 smaller potatoes** (russets or Yukon Golds, whatever is on hand), cut them into chunks and place in a pot of cold, well-salted water. Bring to a boil and cook until very tender then drain well and mash with **2 tablespoons butter** and **about 1 cup whole milk** until smooth. Slice **4 carrots,** put in a saucepan with **½ cup water** and simmer over moderately high heat until the carrots are tender and the water has mostly evaporated, about 10 minutes. Add the chopped meat and onions and cook until warmed through. Season with **salt and black pepper** to taste. Remove from the heat and stir in **1 cup frozen peas**. Spread the mixture in a gratin dish and top with the mashed potatoes. Bake in a 400°F oven until the top is golden brown and the mixture is heated through, 20 to 25 minutes.

RAJAS CON CREMA SERVES 4 TO 6

We like to fold this creamy tangle of onions and roasted poblano chiles into warm corn tortillas, but rajas also make a delicious side dish with roast chicken, grilled steak or sausages. Serve any leftovers with fried eggs for breakfast. If you can't find crema at your local Mexican bodega or grocery store, heavy cream can be substituted, though the result may be a touch less voluptuous.

In August, when corn is at its sweetest, we make Rajas con Elote: cut the kernels from two ears and add them to the skillet with the roasted poblano strips. Increase the amount of crema to $1\frac{1}{4}$ cups.

6 poblano chiles

2 tablespoons olive oil

1 large white onion, cut into ½-inch wedges

Kosher salt and freshly ground black pepper

¾ cup crema

¼ cup finely crumbled queso fresco

ROAST THE WHOLE CHILES UNTIL BLACKENED all over—you can do this on a grill, directly on the grates of a gas stove or under the broiler. Depending on the method you use, blackening the chiles will take 5 to 15 minutes. As they are done, drop them into a paper bag and close up to steam. You can also place them in a bowl and cover tightly with plastic wrap.

Remove the cooled chiles from the bag and peel off as much of the blackened skin as you can. Don't worry if you can't get it all, but don't be tempted to rush the job by running the chiles under cold water—you'll rinse away much of their flavor. Cut out the stems and remove the seeds. Cut or tear the chiles into wide strips.

Combine the oil and onions in a medium heavy skillet over moderate heat and cook, stirring from time to time, until the onions are softened, about 8 minutes. Add the poblano strips and season with ½ teaspoon salt and several grinds of black pepper. Stir in the crema, reduce the heat to low and simmer until the chiles and onions are tender, about 8 minutes. Remove from the heat and stir in the queso fresco. Serve warm.

PICO DE GALLO MAKES ABOUT 2 CUPS

Salsa made at the peak of tomato season is the ideal, but a homemade salsa using inferior tomatoes will still be better than any refrigerated "fresh" salsas from the supermarket, which often contain sugar and citric acid. Most shelf-stable jarred varieties have their own time and place—namely on the floor of a dorm room at 1:30 in the morning. Before adding the jalapeño, taste it—they can vary drastically in heat and flavor. Much of their heat is concentrated in the ribs and seeds, so go with your tastes, adding more or less as you like.

1 large ripe tomato, cored and chopped
½ medium white onion, finely chopped
1 jalapeño, finely chopped
¼ cup finely chopped cilantro
Kosher salt

PUT TOMATOES, ONIONS, JALAPEÑOS AND cilantro in a bowl and season with ½ teaspoon salt. Stir gently to combine. Serve with tortilla chips, on tacos or quesadillas, over grilled meats, or with eggs.

CHIMAYÓ RED CHILE SAUCE
MAKES ABOUT 6 CUPS

We lived in Santa Fe for many years, and there is much that we miss—the big sky, relaxed lifestyle, dear friends and certainly the food, especially the abundance of red and green chiles, which are served on *everything*. We're thrilled that growers in Hatch, New Mexico, have been finding a wider audience for their incredible green chiles. Our local supermarket in New Jersey even hosts a chile roasting event each fall that almost replicates the feel of September in northern New Mexico, when every parking lot boasts a roaster and the air is filled with the perfume of charred chiles. Dried New Mexico red chiles—the best of which come from Chimayó, a tiny town in a valley of the Sangre de Cristo mountains—have not yet had their national moment, but we think it's only a matter of time. Until then, frequent visits and good mail-order sites have allowed us to replicate the taste we love. We keep this sauce on hand to spoon over breakfast burritos, pinto beans and Frito pies.

2 yellow onions, coarsely chopped

4 plump garlic cloves, coarsely chopped

3 tablespoons olive oil

1¼ cups New Mexico red chile powder

6 cups water

1 teaspoon dried oregano

Kosher salt

COMBINE THE ONIONS AND GARLIC IN A FOOD processor and pulse until finely chopped, almost puréed. Heat the olive oil in a heavy pot over moderately high heat. Add the onion slurry and cook, stirring occasionally, until softened and very fragrant, about 5 minutes. Add the chile powder and stir until a thick, smooth paste forms. Add the water, oregano and 1½ teaspoons kosher salt. Bring to a boil, then reduce the heat to moderately low and simmer until the sauce has darkened and thickened slightly, about 30 minutes.

Use immediately or remove from the heat and cool completely before refrigerating or freezing. Stored in an airtight container, the sauce will keep in the fridge for about 2 weeks and for many months in the freezer.

NEW MEXICO–STYLE RED CHILE ENCHILADAS SERVES 6

When we land in Albuquerque, the first thing on our minds is where we'll stop to get enchiladas. Our favorite spots serve cheese enchiladas like these alongside a juicy grilled steak—add a margarita and it's hard to imagine that life could get much better.

1 pound Monterey Jack cheese, shredded

6 ounces goat cheese

1 large white onion, finely chopped

Vegetable oil, for frying

18 corn tortillas

About 3 cups Chimayó Red Chile Sauce (page 72), at room temperature

Shredded lettuce, chopped tomatoes and chopped scallions, for serving

COMBINE THE MONTEREY JACK AND GOAT cheeses in a bowl with the onion. Use a fork to mash the mixture together, then set aside.

Heat about ¼ inch vegetable oil in a medium skillet over moderately high heat. When the oil shimmers, add 1 tortilla at a time, holding it under the oil with tongs until just softened, 10 to 15 seconds. Use the tongs to remove the tortilla, letting any excess oil drip back into the skillet before transferring it to a plate. Repeat with the remaining tortillas, stacking them on the plate as you go.

Once you have fried all the tortillas, heat the oven to 400°F. Organize your work surface: Line up the fried tortillas, red chile sauce and cheese mixture in front of you, as well as a plate on which to roll the enchiladas and a large gratin dish. Dip 1 fried tortilla into the chile sauce, letting the excess drip back into the bowl. Lay the tortilla on the plate. Spread about ¼ cup of the cheese mixture down the middle of the tortilla. Roll the tortilla snugly around the filling then place it, seam side down, in the gratin dish. Continue with the remaining tortillas and cheese, arranging the enchiladas closely together in the dish. Pour the remaining chile sauce over the enchiladas, leaving the ends bare so that they crisp up in the oven.

Bake, uncovered, until the cheese is bubbling and the edges of the tortillas are crisp, 12 to 15 minutes. Remove from the oven and top with the lettuce, tomatoes and scallions. Serve hot.

SHRIMP TOSTADAS MAKES 12 TOSTADAS

The whole menu at Marisco's La Playa, a Mexican seafood restaurant in Santa Fe, is fantastic, but we always end up ordering at least one plate of the shrimp ceviche tostadas—they're just too good. This is our humble approximation, which we've come to love as much as the original. It's a great dinner party dish—colorful, fun and festive.

1½ pounds medium shrimp, peeled and deveined

¾ cup freshly squeezed lime juice

Kosher salt

3 plum tomatoes, seeded and finely chopped

1 small white onion, finely chopped

1 small cucumber, peeled, seeded and finely chopped

1 to 2 jalapeños, finely chopped

3 tablespoons finely chopped cilantro

2 avocados

Vegetable oil, for frying

12 corn tortillas

½ cup mayonnaise

BRING A POT OF SALTED WATER TO A BOIL. Add the shrimp and poach for 1 minute. Drain well. When the shrimp are cool enough to handle, coarsely chop them and place in a bowl. Add ½ cup lime juice to the shrimp, season with salt and toss to coat.

Add the tomatoes, onions, cucumber, jalapeños and cilantro to the shrimp and toss together gently. Season with more salt and lime juice to taste. Refrigerate the mixture until ready to serve.

Pit, peel and dice the avocados, mixing them gently with about 3 tablespoons lime juice. Season with salt to taste.

Line a large platter with paper towels or newspaper. Heat a thin layer of oil in a small heavy skillet over moderately high heat. Fry 1 tortilla at a time, holding it under the oil with tongs and flipping it halfway through, until golden brown and beginning to crisp, about 2 minutes total. Transfer to the lined platter to drain; the tortillas will crisp up as they cool, transforming into tostadas. Repeat with the remaining tortillas.

To assemble, spread each tostada with a spoonful of mayonnaise. Give the shrimp mixture a stir and scoop a big heap of it onto each tostada. Top with some of the diced avocado and serve at once.

BISTEC PALOMILLO SERVES 4 TO 6

Kate grew up eating versions of this dish in little Cuban restaurants in the Florida Keys where she spent childhood summers. The combination of juicy steak and tangy onions, usually served with bowls of yellow rice and black beans, always satisfied. It still does.

2 pounds skirt steak

Kosher salt and freshly ground black pepper

1 large white onion, thinly sliced into rings

4 plump garlic cloves, finely chopped

Freshly squeezed juice of 2 limes

1 tablespoon olive oil

Handful of cilantro leaves

CUT THE STEAK INTO 4 TO 6 EQUAL PIECES and season well all over with salt and pepper. Combine the steak, onions, garlic and lime juice in a large resealable plastic bag. Seal the bag, pressing out as much air as you can, and squish everything together to combine. Let the steak marinate in the fridge, set in a shallow pan or bowl, for at least 1 hour and up to overnight.

Remove the steaks from the bag (reserve the marinade), brushing off any onions and garlic that stick to the meat. Pat the steaks dry with paper towels and season again with salt and pepper.

Heat a very large heavy skillet over high heat until almost smoking. Swirl in the olive oil, then add the steaks and sear until the undersides are crusted and well browned, 3 to 4 minutes. Flip and cook another 3 to 4 minutes for medium-rare, removing any thinner pieces as they are done. Transfer the steaks to a platter to rest.

Add the reserved marinade, onions and garlic to the skillet and cook, stirring occasionally, until the mixture is bubbling hard and the onions are crisp-tender, 3 to 4 minutes. Scrape the onions and sauce over the steaks. Scatter some cilantro over everything and serve at once.

BLACK BEANS SERVES 6

Beans from scratch are a staple in our house (but we admit to the guilty pleasure of buying packages of Vigo yellow rice). They are so cheap, so easy to make and so very good. Put **1 pound dried black beans** in a heavy pot and cover completely with cold water. Set aside overnight to soak. The next day, add enough fresh cold water so that the beans are covered by 2 inches. Add **1 halved yellow onion, 2 plump garlic cloves, 1 bay leaf, 1 dried red chile** and **1 tablespoon ground cumin**. Bring the mixture to a boil then reduce the heat to moderately low and simmer gently, stirring from time to time, until the beans are almost tender, about 45 minutes.

Add **2 finely chopped garlic cloves** to the beans, along with **1 tablespoon distilled white vinegar, 1 tablespoon olive oil** and **1 tablespoon kosher salt**. Continue to cook the beans until completely tender, about 15 minutes more. Remove from the heat. Pluck out the onion halves, whole garlic cloves, bay leaf and dried chile. Taste and adjust the seasonings, adding a little more salt if needed.

IN THE PINK
RED ONIONS

Red Onions. It's not nice to play favorites, but we can't help having a soft spot for red onions. Maybe it's nostalgia for our months living in Sicily, when we cooked exclusively with local red onions. Or maybe it's even more superficial. With their concentric rings of purple skin and ivory flesh, red onions are just so darn pretty. We fall for them every time.

Their flavor is not especially different from other storage onions—assertive when raw, they sweeten up with cooking—and they can be used interchangeably, but we always reach for a red when we want a pop of brightness. That color fades a bit when cooked, but it comes to vibrant, fluorescent life with pickling. Opening the fridge and seeing a jar of pickled red onions always gives us hope for our next meal, whatever it may be. When perusing a seed catalog, the red onions will jump right out at you, with names like Red Baron, Red Zeppelin, Red Bull, Red Wing, Purplette and Cabernet. Depending on the variety, they can vary in shape from globes to torpedoes and in size from small as a golf ball to large enough to completely cover a half-pound burger. Now doesn't that sound good?

RED ONION GOAT CHEESE GALETTE SERVES 6

Form, function and flavor go hand in hand in hand in this pretty little free-form tart. The scallion goat cheese base is an easy layer of flavor. It's also one of our favorite combos to spread on crackers.

FOR THE DOUGH

1½ cups all-purpose flour

Kosher salt

8 tablespoons cold butter, cut into pieces

3 to 4 tablespoons ice water

FOR THE FILLING

4 medium red onions

2 tablespoons olive oil

Kosher salt and freshly ground black pepper

1 bunch scallions, finely chopped

4 ounces goat cheese

TO MAKE THE DOUGH, COMBINE THE FLOUR and ¼ teaspoon salt in a bowl and, using your hands or a pastry cutter, quickly work in the butter, squeezing or cutting it until the floury mixture is filled with pea-sized lumps. Drizzle 3 tablespoons ice water over the mixture and stir together with your hands or a fork until it will just hold together when squeezed. Add the remaining water if you need it. Gather the dough into a ball and flatten slightly, then wrap well in plastic wrap. Refrigerate for at least 1 hour and up to 2 days; the dough can also be frozen for up to 1 month.

To make the filling, peel the onions, neatly trim the root end and cut them lengthwise into ½-inch wedges, keeping the root end intact so they hold together.

Heat the olive oil in a skillet over moderate heat. Arrange as many onion wedges as will fit in a single layer in the skillet and season with salt and pepper. Cook the onions, without stirring or moving them, until the bottoms are nicely browned, about 5 minutes. Spoon the onions onto a plate, taking care not to break them up, but not worrying about it if you do. Repeat with the remaining onions.

Combine the scallions and goat cheese in a bowl and mash together with a fork until very well combined. Season to taste with salt and pepper.

Heat the oven to 400°F. Line a baking sheet with parchment or a Silpat.

Roll the dough into a 12-inch round on a lightly floured countertop, then transfer it to the baking sheet. Spread the goat cheese mixture evenly over the dough, leaving a 2-inch border. Arrange the onions, browned sides up, over the cheese, then fold the edges of the dough over, pleating as necessary.

Bake the galette until the pastry is golden brown, about 40 minutes. Remove from the oven and serve warm or at room temperature.

SFINCIONE SERVES 8

This is typical street fare in Palermo, a thick, oily pizza dough topped with a mess of tomatoes, onions and anchovies that is meant to tide you over until your next meal. The first sfincione we tasted spoiled us forever—it was made by Giovanna Pacino, the exacting, no-nonsense kitchen manager at the Anna Tasca Lanza School of Sicilian Cooking in Vallelunga, where we lived and worked for several months. Giovanna's tender dough was topped judiciously with the farm's own onions, blanched briefly to cut their bite, plus homemade tomato sauce and plenty of local Pecorino—delicious with a glass of the family's cool white wine. How could Palermo's food carts stand a chance?

FOR THE TOPPING

2 red onions, thinly sliced

1½ cups good-quality tomato sauce

1 cup lightly toasted bread crumbs

1 cup freshly grated Pecorino

6 oil-packed anchovies, finely chopped

1 teaspoon dried oregano, preferably wild

3 tablespoons olive oil, divided

FOR THE DOUGH

3 cups all-purpose flour

⅔ cup semolina flour

2 teaspoons yeast

2 teaspoons sugar

Kosher salt

1 cup warm water

2 tablespoons olive oil

TO MAKE THE TOPPING, BRING A SMALL POT of water to a boil. Add the onions and blanch for 1 minute. Drain well.

Combine the tomato sauce, bread crumbs, Pecorino, anchovies, oregano and 2 tablespoons olive oil in a bowl. Add the drained onions and stir together. Set aside while you make the dough.

To make the dough, combine the all-purpose flour, semolina flour, yeast, sugar and 1 teaspoon salt in a large bowl and whisk together with your hands. Make a well in the center of the mixture and add the warm water and olive oil. Using your hands, stir the wet ingredients into the dry until it comes together into a shaggy dough. Scoop the dough out onto a lightly floured work surface and knead by hand until very smooth. This should take 8 to 10 minutes.

Lightly oil a 9x13-inch cake pan. Plop the dough into the pan and gently stretch it to fill the pan. If it resists, let it rest for a few minutes before working on it some more. Spread the onion topping evenly over the dough so that it is completely covered. Drizzle the remaining 1 tablespoon olive oil over the topping. Cover the pan with a clean kitchen towel and let rise until doubled in size, about 2 hours.

Heat the oven to 350°F. Bake the pizza until the crust is puffed and golden and the topping is juicy, 40 to 45 minutes. Remove from the oven and let cool slightly before cutting into big squares for serving. Sfincione is equally good at room temperature or even cold the next day.

RED ONION DOSAS WITH COCONUT CHUTNEY SERVES 6 TO 8

We ate our first dosas—South Indian fermented pancakes—in the Jackson Heights neighborhood of Queens, and their light, crisp texture and accompanying array of simple chutneys has held our imagination ever since. When we make our own, we often serve them alone with this chutney, but they can be filled like crêpes with roasted cauliflower, lentils or curried potatoes for a perfect vegetarian dinner. Sometimes labeled black lentils, urad dal is available a number of ways, both with and without their ebony skins. For this dish, seek out skinned and split urad dal, which are creamy white. They are sold at Indian grocery stores, where you can also find the fresh curry leaves. Note that the dosa batter needs to ferment for at least 8 hours, so plan accordingly.

FOR THE DOSAS

1½ cups long-grain white rice

¾ cup split urad dal

Kosher salt

1 red onion, finely chopped

1 fresh green chile, finely chopped

1-inch piece fresh ginger, finely chopped

Vegetable oil, for frying

½ teaspoon brown mustard seeds

6 to 8 fresh curry leaves, finely chopped

1 teaspoon cumin seeds

FOR THE CHUTNEY

1 cup shredded or flaked unsweetened coconut

1 fresh green chile, coarsely chopped

½-inch piece fresh ginger, coarsely chopped

½ cup cilantro leaves

1 cup plain whole-milk yogurt

1½ tablespoons freshly squeezed lemon juice

Kosher salt

1 tablespoon vegetable oil

½ teaspoon brown mustard seeds

3 to 4 fresh curry leaves

START MAKING THE DOSAS THE DAY BEFORE you want to serve them. Place the rice and urad dal in separate bowls and cover each with cold water by 2 inches. Set aside to soak at room temperature for 4 hours.

Drain the rice and place in a food processor with ⅓ cup cold water. Process until pasty, about 1 minute. Scrape the mixture into a large bowl; don't worry about cleaning it out. Drain the urad dal and place in the food processor. Add 1½ cups cold water and blend until smooth and creamy, about 2 minutes. Add to the bowl of rice and stir in 1 teaspoon salt. Cover the bowl with plastic wrap and set aside in a warm place to ferment overnight or up to 24 hours.

The next day, stir the red onion, green chile and ginger into the dosa batter, along with 1 cup water and ¼ teaspoon salt. Heat ½ teaspoon vegetable oil in a small skillet over moderately high heat. When the oil is hot, add the mustard seeds. They will immediately start crackling and popping—cover the pan to keep the seeds from escaping—and fry for 30 seconds or so. Add the curry leaves and cumin seeds and fry for just a few seconds. Scrape this spice mixture into the dosa batter and stir well to combine. Cover the bowl again with plastic wrap and set aside for another 2 hours.

CONTINUED

While the batter rests, make the chutney. Combine the coconut, green chile and ginger in a food processor and pulse until the mixture is very finely chopped. Add the cilantro, yogurt, lemon juice and 1 teaspoon salt and blend until smooth and very well combined. The coconut will not break down completely, but you want that bit of texture. Transfer the chutney to a bowl and refrigerate, covered with plastic wrap, until ready to serve the dosas.

To cook the dosas, heat a medium nonstick or cast-iron skillet over moderate heat. Pour 1 teaspoon vegetable oil into the skillet and tilt the skillet to coat lightly (or spread it around with a paper towel). Fill a ⅓ cup measure with batter and pour into the heated skillet. Working quickly, use the back of a spoon to spread the batter thinly over the entire skillet; don't worry if there are a few gaps or lacy edges. Drizzle the dosa with another

1 teaspoon oil and cook until the underside is golden and crisp, about 2 minutes. Flip the dosa and continue to cook, pressing down lightly with a spatula, until the second side is pale golden, about 1 minute more. Transfer the dosa to a platter and keep warm, loosely covered with foil, while you continue making more. Remember to oil the skillet between batches.

Just before serving, finish the chutney. Heat the coconut oil in a small skillet over moderately high heat. Add the mustard seeds and cover the pan while they crackle and pop, about 30 seconds. Remove the lid and drop in the curry leaves and fry until they are crisp and bright green. This will only take a couple of seconds. Remove from the heat and pour the spice mixture over the chutney.

To serve, loosely roll up the warm dosas and serve with the chutney.

ONION FRITTATA WITH SHERRY VINEGAR SERVES 4 TO 6

This frittata, adapted closely from a recipe by Deborah Madison, is a favorite of ours. A splash of sherry vinegar keeps the soft golden onions from sliding into their too-sweet spot.

2 pounds red or yellow onions, chopped

2 tablespoons olive oil

2 tablespoons sherry vinegar

Kosher salt and freshly ground black pepper

6 large eggs, lightly beaten

2 tablespoons butter

1 tablespoon chopped flat-leaf parsley

COMBINE THE ONIONS AND OLIVE OIL IN A large nonstick skillet and cook over moderate heat, stirring occasionally, until the onions are soft and golden, 30 to 35 minutes. Stir in 1 tablespoon vinegar and season with ½ teaspoon salt and several grinds of black pepper.

Pour the eggs evenly over the onions. Using a spatula, gently push the eggs toward the center of the pan, letting the raw egg flow underneath and taking care to keep the onions in as even a layer as possible. Continue cooking until the underside of the frittata is set. When the frittata is almost cooked through, carefully slide it onto a plate. Invert the pan over the plate and flip so the frittata is cooked-side up. Cook for another minute or two until cooked through. Slide the frittata onto a serving plate.

Return the skillet to the heat and add the butter. When it has melted and foamed, swirl in the remaining 1 tablespoon vinegar. Drizzle the mixture over the top of the frittata and scatter with the parsley. Serve warm.

MILK-BRAISED RED ONION FRITTATA SERVES 4 TO 6

One August, we were lucky enough to spend two weeks with Mary Taylor Simeti, the American-born author who has called Sicily home for fifty-odd years. This interesting frittata, in which onions are simmered in milk before the eggs are added, was one of many recipes we picked up from her family. Its looks leave a little to be desired—the onions cook down to a pinkish gray, so a garnish of chopped herbs works wonders—but the flavor and custardy texture are a treat.

Thinly slice **2 red onions** and put in a medium nonstick skillet. Add **1 cup whole milk** and bring to a boil over moderately high heat. Cook, stirring every now and then, until the onions are soft and the milk has almost completely evaporated, leaving behind soft curds, about 10 minutes. Meanwhile, lightly beat **4 large eggs** with **½ teaspoon kosher salt** and several grinds of **black pepper**. Pour the eggs evenly into the skillet. Using a spatula, gently push the eggs toward the center of the pan, letting the raw egg flow underneath. When the frittata is almost cooked through, carefully slide it onto a plate. Invert the skillet over the plate and flip so the frittata is cooked-side up. Cook for another few minutes until cooked through. Slide onto a serving platter, garnish with chopped herbs, and serve warm or cold.

INSALATA TROPEANA SERVES 2 TO 4

One August, as we drove down the coast of Calabria on our way to Sicily, we thrilled at the sight of long braids of purple Tropea onions hanging from every roadside *verdure* stand. The area is justly famous for its mild torpedo-shaped onions, and versions of this salad are available everywhere. When we returned home, we were so happy to discover that one of our local New Jersey farms has had great success growing Tropea onions, which we eagerly snapped up so we could continue making this wonderful salad.

2 small red onions, preferably Tropea

4 ripe tomatoes, cored and sliced

½ teaspoon dried oregano

Kosher salt and freshly ground black pepper

2 tablespoons olive oil

Handful of mint leaves

SLICE THE ONIONS AS THINLY AS POSSIBLE, preferably using a mandoline, and arrange them on a large platter. Lay the sliced tomatoes over the onions (their juices will soften the bite of the raw onions).

Crumble the dried oregano between your fingers and sprinkle over the tomatoes. Season with ¼ teaspoon salt and a few grinds of black pepper. Drizzle the olive oil over the tomatoes and onions and scatter the mint leaves over top, tearing any large ones into smaller pieces.

TOMATO, CUCUMBER AND RED ONION SALAD SERVES 3 TO 4

We eat a version of this salad weekly when tomatoes are in season, often paired with grilled skirt steak and corn on the cob. Sometimes we bring the salad to the table with a stack of toasted bread and a jar of mayonnaise, then go to town making juicy tomato sandwiches. On a hot August night, adding fresh mozzarella turns the salad into a complete meal.

Thinly slice **1 small red onion** and season with **1 tablespoon sherry vinegar, ½ teaspoon kosher salt** and **several grinds of black pepper**. Add **4 tablespoons good olive oil** and stir together. Peel **1 cucumber** (remove the seeds if you like) and slice into thin rounds. Stir into the onion mixture. Core a **few juicy-ripe tomatoes** (1 large tomato per person or several smaller tomatoes; this always looks great with a mixture of colorful heirloom varieties). Slice into rounds if large or wedges if smaller. Cherry or grape tomatoes can be halved. Arrange the tomatoes on a large platter and season lightly with salt and pepper. Spoon the cucumber and onion mixture over the tomatoes and let sit at room temperature for a few minutes before serving.

LENTIL SALAD 101 SERVES 4 TO 6

This hearty salad, which we make several times a month to keep in the fridge as a basis for easy lunches, often includes whatever we have on hand. Think of this recipe simply as a template: We may sub in chopped scallions for the onion, add a little curry powder or cumin, fold in a handful of chopped apples, carrot, or fennel, or crumble some feta or ricotta salata over it. Sometimes we use fresh lemon juice in place of the vinegar, and sometimes we add no acid at all.

1½ cups small green lentils, such as le Puy

1 red, yellow or white onion, halved lengthwise

1 carrot

3 celery ribs

1 garlic clove

1 bay leaf

Kosher salt

3 tablespoons olive oil

2 tablespoons red wine vinegar

2 tablespoons finely chopped flat-leaf parsley

Freshly ground black pepper

PICK THROUGH THE LENTILS THEN TRANSFER to a large saucepan. Add one onion half to the saucepan and reserve the other. Cut the carrot and 1 of the celery ribs into large chunks and add to the saucepan, along with the garlic clove, bay leaf and 1 teaspoon salt. Add enough water to cover the lentils by 2 inches, then bring to a boil. Reduce the heat to moderate and simmer until the lentils are tender, 20 to 25 minutes. Drain well and pluck out the onion, celery, carrot, garlic and bay leaf from the lentils and discard.

While the lentils are simmering, finely chop the remaining onion half and celery ribs; transfer to a large bowl. Add the lentils, stir in the oil, vinegar and parsley and season to taste with salt and pepper. Serve the lentils at room temperature, tasting them again just before serving and adjusting the seasonings as needed.

TURKISH ONION AND PARSLEY SALAD SERVES 2 TO 4

We serve this dead-simple salad with Grilled Lamb Chops Two Ways (page 304) or as part of a meze platter with spiced chickpeas or hummus, but honestly, its bright, tart flavors work well with almost anything. The onions here are grilled just long enough to amp up their sweetness and color. The salad's beauty, deliciousness and ease exemplify all that we love about Middle Eastern cooking.

2 medium red onions

2 tablespoons olive oil

Kosher salt and freshly ground black pepper

Leaves from 1 bunch flat-leaf parsley

1 tablespoon freshly squeezed lemon juice

2 teaspoons ground sumac

CUT THE ONIONS INTO BITE-SIZED WEDGES. Thread the onion wedges onto skewers, leaving a little space between each so they cook evenly. If using bamboo skewers, make sure to soak the skewers in water for 30 minutes or so before threading so they don't go up in flames on the grill.

Brush the skewered onions with 1 tablespoon olive oil and season with salt and pepper. Grill over high heat until the onions are charred in spots, turning occasionally so they cook more or less evenly, 3 to 4 minutes. Alternatively, run the skewers under the broiler or use a stovetop grill pan.

Toss the parsley leaves with the lemon juice and remaining 1 tablespoon olive oil. Season with salt and pepper. Remove the onions from the skewers and toss with the parsley salad. Sprinkle the sumac over everything and serve at once.

ONION AND SUMAC RELISH MAKES ABOUT ½ CUP

The flavors of the salad above also work harmoniously in a fresh relish. In this case, all the tartness comes from ground sumac. Sprinkle it over grilled steak, chicken, lamb, roasted vegetables or summer-ripe tomatoes. Stir together **1 finely chopped red onion, 1 tablespoon ground sumac** and **¼ teaspoon kosher salt**. Stir in **6 tablespoons finely chopped parsley**. Let sit for an hour or so before serving.

ESCAROLE SALAD WITH ORANGES AND RED ONION SERVES 4 TO 6

We ate a version of this salad several times a week the winter we lived in Sicily. The oranges were plucked from the grove out front, chicory and fennel pulled from the garden and onions retrieved from the shed where they had been cured and stored. The combination of sweet and bitter, accented by the onion's sharp bite, is very refreshing, especially against the rich meats and stews of the colder months. We still make it often, finding the ingredients we need at our local ShopRite. Less romantic, to be sure, but just as satisfying. Many cooks prefer to use only the tender, pale inner leaves of the head of escarole to make a salad. If we are feeling very refined, we follow that lead. Otherwise, we only discard the very toughest outer leaves and enjoy everything else.

1 small red onion, thinly sliced

3 navel oranges

1 head escarole

1 fennel bulb, cored and thinly sliced

1 tablespoon freshly squeezed lemon juice

1 tablespoon red wine vinegar

Kosher salt and freshly ground black pepper

3 tablespoons olive oil

½ teaspoon dried oregano, optional

PUT THE SLICED ONIONS IN A SMALL BOWL. Using a sharp knife, cut off all of the orange peel and pith and then, working over the bowl of onions to collect the juice, cut the orange segments free from the membranes, letting the fruit drop into the bowl of onions. Squeeze the orange "carcasses" over the bowl to wring out a few last drops of juice. Let the onions and oranges sit (the juice will soften the heat of the onions) while you prepare the rest of the salad.

Wash and dry the escarole well, then tear the leaves into bite-sized pieces and put in a salad bowl. Add the fennel to the escarole then season the salad with ½ teaspoon salt and several grinds of black pepper.

Drain the onions and oranges, reserving the juice. Measure out 1 tablespoon of the orange juice and add to the salad, along with the lemon juice, vinegar and olive oil. Toss everything together to coat with dressing. Taste and adjust the seasonings as needed. Scatter the onions and oranges on top and toss together very gently so that they are evenly strewn throughout the salad. If you like, sprinkle with the oregano and serve at once.

RED ONION BLOSSOMS MAKES 6

These roasted blooms just might be the prettiest dish in this book. Inspired by a recipe from chef Laurent Tourondel, they are also one of the simplest and most delicious. Serve the blossoms alone with some crusty bread as a statement piece, or place them atop a steak or salad and drizzle their tangy juices over everything.

6 medium red onions

6 tablespoons white balsamic vinegar

6 tablespoons olive oil

Kosher salt and freshly ground black pepper

HEAT THE OVEN TO 425°F. USING A SHARP knife, trim ¼ inch off the top of each onion. Trim the root, but leave it intact. Peel the onions then cut each one lengthwise into eighths, stopping about ½ inch from the bottom so the onion stays intact.

Lay a large square of heavy-duty foil on a shallow bowl. Put 1 onion, root end down, on top of the foil. Drizzle with 1 tablespoon each of the balsamic vinegar and olive oil, then season well with salt and pepper. Fold up the foil and pinch the edges to seal the packet. Repeat with the remaining onions to make 6 packets.

Place the wrapped onions on a sheet pan and roast until the onions are tender when pierced with a skewer, 25 to 30 minutes. Unwrap the onions and let them cool slightly before carefully transferring them to plates. They will open naturally into a flower shape. Drizzle any of the juices that have collected in the foil over the onions. Season with a bit more salt and pepper and serve warm.

PICKLED RED ONIONS MAKES 1 QUART

If you try only one recipe in this book, let it be this one. We put these vivid onions on everything from tacos to salads to steak to pizza to eggs to beans and rice. They are a delicious addition to avocado toast, and they make almost anything taste a little brighter, a little better. There's nothing worse than building a beautiful BLT then discovering there are no pickled onions in the fridge, so when we see our jar getting low, we get to work—which takes all of five minutes—and make another. You can tuck in a dried chile or a sprinkle of oregano, but our go-to version is down and dirty—just onions, white vinegar and salt.

4 medium red onions

2 cups distilled white vinegar

Kosher salt

PEEL AND QUARTER THE ONIONS LENGTH-wise, then cut crosswise into thin slices. As you work, pack the onions into a clean quart jar until it is full.

Combine the vinegar and 2 teaspoons salt in a saucepan and bring to a boil, stirring until the salt is dissolved. Pour the boiling vinegar over the onions, pressing down to keep them submerged. Let the mixture cool before you seal the jar and refrigerate. The onions should rest overnight before you serve them. They will keep for a month or more in the fridge but rarely last that long.

CITRUS-PICKLED ONIONS MAKES ABOUT 2 CUPS

A little sweeter than other pickle recipes in this book, the citrus here plays well with fatty, lip-smacking meats like Cuban Pork Roast (page 323). You can make this with all white onions, but the red onion adds some pretty color. These will keep 3 to 5 days in the fridge. Quarter **1 large white onion** and **1 small red onion** lengthwise, slice thinly and transfer to a bowl. Add the freshly squeezed juice of **2 oranges** and **2 limes**. Stir in **½ teaspoon dried oregano** and **¾ teaspoon kosher salt**. Refrigerate for at least 2 hours before serving, giving a stir every now and then.

FERMENTED RED ONIONS MAKES ABOUT 2 CUPS

Onions fermented in a brine of just salt and water develop a funkier but more gentle twang than vinegar-pickled onions. Use these just as you would the Pickled Red Onions (page 104).

2 medium red onions, thinly sliced

2 small dried red chiles, such as *chile de arbol*

1½ cups warm water

Kosher salt

PACK THE SLICED ONIONS AND DRIED CHILES into a clean pint jar. Stir together the warm water and 1 tablespoon salt until the salt is dissolved. Pour the brine over the onions, pressing down on them so they are completely submerged.

Fill a small plastic bag with enough water so that it will sit comfortably in the mouth of the jar, pressing down on the onions to keep them submerged in the brine. Tuck this set-up in a cool room temperature spot for 5 days. On the fifth day, taste an onion. If it is tangy enough for your tastes, seal the jar and stick in the refrigerator. If you want a little more fizz and flavor, let it sit out for another day or two before sealing and refrigerating. The onions will keep for a month or so in the fridge.

RED, RED JAM MAKES ABOUT 2 CUPS

Inky and lustrous, this red onion jam begs to be paired with duck breasts, venison and juicy pork chops. A thin layer elevates a grilled cheese sandwich to the heavens, or tuck it between buttered toast with some thick-cut bacon. We've been known to stand over the stove and just eat forkfuls straight from the skillet. Not ashamed.

3 tablespoons olive oil

4 medium red onions, thinly sliced

Kosher salt and freshly ground black pepper

1 sprig fresh rosemary

2 cups dry red wine

½ cup maple syrup, preferably grade B

½ cup red wine vinegar

COMBINE THE OLIVE OIL AND ONIONS IN A large skillet over moderately high heat. Season well with salt and pepper, and cook until the onions begin to soften, about 5 minutes.

While the onions cook, strip the rosemary leaves and chop them. Add to the onions, along with the red wine. Bring the mixture to a simmer then reduce the heat to low and simmer very gently, uncovered, until the wine is almost completely reduced, about 40 minutes.

When the wine is almost reduced, add the maple syrup and vinegar to the onions and continue to simmer gently until the liquid is reduced and the onions are jam-like but still juicy, about 1 hour. Remove from the heat and serve at once. Or, cool completely before refrigerating for up to 2 weeks.

KACHUMBAR
SPICY RED ONION RELISH MAKES ABOUT 3 CUPS

In Hindi, *kacha* means "raw," and kachumbar is a mix of finely chopped fresh vegetables and herbs that helps balance rich foods such as curries, lentils, biryani or roasted meats. Naomi Mobed, the creative force behind a delicious line of chutneys, taught us this recipe, and it's now what we turn to when we crave a break from chips and salsa. (We like to serve it with crisp pappadams.) Kachumbar has found its way into the cuisines of Central as well as East Africa, and the variations are limitless. Naomi suggests adding any combination of finely diced Granny Smith apple, ripe mango, pomelo, pomegranate seeds, green papaya and tomatillos to the mix below.

FOR THE DRESSING

Freshly grated zest of 1 lemon or lime

6 tablespoons freshly squeezed lemon or lime juice

1 tablespoon sugar

¼ teaspoon ground cayenne

⅛ teaspoon ground turmeric

Kosher salt

FOR THE SALAD

½ teaspoon caraway seeds

½ teaspoon cumin seeds

½ teapoon fennel seeds

1 large red onion, finely chopped

1 large ripe tomato, cored and finely chopped

1 small Persian cucumber, finely diced

4 radishes, finely chopped

1 to 2 fresh green chiles, such as jalapeño or serrano, finely chopped

3 tablespoons finely chopped cilantro

1 tablespoon finely chopped fresh mint

1 tablespoon finely chopped or grated fresh ginger

½ teaspoon dried mint

TO MAKE THE DRESSING, WHISK TOGETHER the lemon or lime zest and juice, the sugar, cayenne, turmeric and ½ teaspoon salt. Set aside.

To make the salad, combine the caraway, cumin and fennel seeds in a small skillet and toast over moderate heat, swirling the skillet to keep the seeds from scorching, until fragrant and a shade darker, about 2 minutes. Remove from the heat.

Combine the onion, tomato, cucumber, radishes, green chiles, cilantro, fresh mint, ginger and dried mint in a bowl. Add the toasted spices and the dressing and stir together gently. Before serving, refrigerate the kachumbar for at least 1 hour for the flavors to come together.

CHICKEN AND CHICKPEAS WITH PRESERVED LEMON RELISH SERVES 4 TO 6

When we discovered the deliciousness of preserved lemons—and started making them by the half-gallon jug—we went overboard and put them in everything: salads, stews, pastas, risottos, even desserts. Our friends are probably happy that we have sailed through that phase. That said, we still crave their singular briny tartness from time to time, and this beautiful sheet pan supper fulfills that hunger and more.

1 (3- to 4-pound) chicken

Kosher salt and freshly ground black pepper

⅓ cup whole-milk yogurt

1 tablespoon Harissa (page 300)

1 tablespoon olive oil, plus more for drizzling

2 red onions

1 (15-ounce) can chickpeas, rinsed and drained

½ cup green olives, such as Picholine or Castel-vetrano, pitted and chopped

Rind of ½ preserved lemon, finely chopped

1 tablespoon chopped flat-leaf parsley

1 tablespoon chopped mint

1 tablespoon freshly squeezed lemon juice

HEAT THE OVEN TO 425°F. BREAK THE chicken down into pieces: 2 drumsticks, 2 thighs, 2 wings and 2 breasts, then cut each breast in half, for quick and even cooking. Freeze the backbone for a future stock. Or, buy about 3 pounds chicken pieces with skin and bone. Season the chicken all over with salt and pepper. Stir together the yogurt and harissa in a large bowl, then add the chicken pieces and stir with your hands to coat.

Drizzle a half-sheet pan with some olive oil. Arrange the drumsticks, thighs and wings (the breasts will go in later) skin side up on the pan. Put in the oven and roast for 15 minutes.

Meanwhile, neatly trim the root ends of the red onions, and cut each onion lengthwise into eighths. Take 2 of the wedges and chop finely; set aside in a bowl.

Add the chickpeas and reserved onion wedges to the bowl with the chicken breasts. Remove the sheet pan from the oven and add the chicken breast pieces to the pan. Scatter the onion wedges, chickpeas and any remaining marinade evenly around the chicken. Return to the oven and roast until the chicken is cooked through (the juices should run clear when the meat is pricked with a knife), about 20 minutes.

While the chicken continues to roast, make the relish. Add the olives, preserved lemon, parsley and mint to the bowl of finely chopped red onion. Stir in the lemon juice and 1 tablespoon olive oil. Season with several grinds of black pepper.

When the chicken is done, remove the pan from the oven and dollop the relish all over the chicken, chickpeas and onions. Gently stir together to coat then transfer to a serving platter and serve warm.

NOTE: For a variation on the theme, substitute a few spoonfuls of Chermoula (page 303) for the preserved lemon, olive and herb mixture.

THE HONEY BUNCH
SWEET ONIONS

Sweet Onions. Fans of sweets claim that they are happy to chomp into raw onions just as they would an apple, but we have yet to see this become common practice. That said, sweet onions are certainly mild enough to be eaten raw in salads and on sandwiches. Their sweetness makes them a natural candidate for caramelizing, and they make great onion rings—their juiciness holds up well in the hot fat.

These onions' characteristic flavor develops from a number of growing conditions. Sulfur is the main factor contributing to the pungency of onions, so growing them in a low-sulfur soil is the first step. The onions must also be well irrigated or planted where they can count on a lot of rain—that added water will further lessen the sulfur in the soil while upping the moisture of the growing onions. The juicier the onion, the milder it will be.

During the nineteenth and early twentieth centuries, the majority of sweet onions enjoyed in the US came from Bermuda. Mark Twain, a frequent visitor to the island, wrote, "The onion is the pride and joy of Bermuda. It is her jewel, her gem of gems. In her conversation, her pulpit, her literature, it is her most frequent and eloquent figure. In Bermuda metaphor it stands for perfection—perfection absolute." Exports ground to a halt during World War I and never fully recovered as Texas farmers began to plant Bermudas in huge quantities. Today, the best-known variety of sweet onion is probably the Vidalia, which, by law, may only be grown in about twenty counties in Georgia and is available from April to August. Also well known are the Walla Walla, which hails from Washington State; Mauis, a smaller variety of sweets from Hawaii; and the 1015, a Texas onion that is named for its ideal planting date of October 15. The Mayan Sweet and Oso Sweet onions from South America keep us in sweets throughout the winter.

Because of their juiciness, sweets are not good keepers. Always handle them gently—they bruise easily, which can make them spoil more quickly—and plan on using them within a couple of days.

SALT-BAKED
SWEET ONIONS SERVES 6

Our friend Ian Knauer, co-owner of the Farm Cooking School in Stockton, New Jersey, is a master of salt-roasting, and his example has encouraged us to try it with onions. The blanket of salt concentrates their flavor—it's a good reminder that onions can be a delicious vegetable in their own right. Serve them with a roast or even a meatloaf, topped with a swirl of the pan juices. A dusting of good grated Parmigiano is also tasty, as is a dollop of Scallion Miso Butter (page 170).

6 sweet onions

4 sprigs fresh thyme

2 cups kosher salt

½ cup water

Butter or olive oil and finely chopped herbs, such as parsley and chives, for serving

HEAT THE OVEN TO 450°F. REMOVE ANY OF the very loose, papery skins from the onions then arrange them in a baking dish; they should just fit, without too much extra space around them. Lay the thyme around the onions. Stir together the salt and water in a bowl—it should have the consistency of wet sand. Pour the salt mixture over and around the onions, pressing with your hands to pack it in—they should look like they are under a layer of glittering snow.

Roast the onions until the salt crust is golden and hardened, 45 minutes to 1 hour. Remove from the oven and, using the back of a heavy knife, crack open the crust. Pull out the onions, discarding the crust and dusting off any of the salt mixture that sticks to them. To serve, split each onion lengthwise and top with a pat of butter or a drizzle of olive oil. Season with salt and pepper and sprinkle with herbs.

VADOUVAN MAKES ABOUT 2 CUPS

This French-Indian spice blend is similar to one developed by Paul Grimes, a former *Gourmet* food editor and ace food stylist. We remember how revolutionary it tasted at the time—frying the alliums then roasting them with lots of spices creates an incredibly resonant flavor. Add a heaping spoonful of vadouvan to rice as it cooks, or to eggs. Fold some into lamb meatballs or create a marinade with yogurt and lime juice for chicken. This is good, good stuff. We've been known to snack on it straight from the baking sheet, like spicy onion brittle.

3 large sweet onions

4 large shallots

6 plump garlic cloves

2 tablespoons peanut or vegetable oil

1½ teaspoons cumin seeds

½ teaspoon coriander seeds

½ teaspoon fenugreek seeds

½ teaspoon brown mustard seeds

½ teaspoon crushed red pepper flakes

¼ teaspoon fennel seeds

3 whole cloves

½ teaspoon ground turmeric

¼ teaspoon freshly grated nutmeg

6 to 8 fresh curry leaves, finely chopped

Kosher salt and freshly ground black pepper

HEAT THE OVEN TO 325°F. PEEL THE ONIONS and cut into big chunks. Pulse in a food processor until coarsely chopped (don't worry if a few large pieces remain) then transfer to a bowl. Peel and quarter the shallots and garlic. Add to the food processor and pulse until coarsely chopped.

Heat the oil in a nonstick skillet over high heat until it shimmers. Add the onions, shallots and garlic and cook, stirring often, until golden and browned in spots, about 15 minutes. Remove from the heat.

While the onions cook, grind the cumin, coriander, fenugreek, mustard seeds, red pepper flakes, fennel and cloves in a spice grinder or use a mortar and pestle. Add the freshly ground spices, turmeric, nutmeg, curry leaves, 1½ teaspoons salt and several grinds of black pepper to the onions and stir well to combine.

Line a sheet pan with parchment or a Silpat. Spread out the onion mixture as thinly and evenly as possible. Bake, stirring every 10 minutes or so with a wooden skewer to help separate the onions, until well browned and barely moist, 45 to 55 minutes. Pay special attention to the onions around the edges to make sure they don't burn.

Scrape the mixture onto a large plate to cool. When the vadouvan is completely cool, transfer to a jar, seal and store in the fridge for up to 1 month or in the freezer for 6 months.

SAVORY VADOUVAN-
SPICED GRANOLA MAKES ABOUT 4½ CUPS

Sprinkle this crunchy mix over salad or eat it out of hand as an afternoon snack. Heat the oven to 350°F. Combine **1 cup rolled oats, ½ cup raw cashews, ½ cup raw pistachios, ½ cup raw sunflower seeds, ½ cup raw pumpkin seeds, ¼ cup raw sesame seeds** and **½ cup Vadouvan** (page 117) in a large bowl. Stir in **⅓ cup melted coconut oil, 1 large egg white, 1 tablespoon honey, ¼ teaspoon cayenne** and **1 teaspoon kosher salt** and toss to combine. Spread the mixture out in a rimmed baking sheet and bake, stirring once, until golden brown and toasted, 25 to 30 minutes. Remove from the oven and stir in **½ cup golden raisins**. Once the granola has cooled completely, transfer it to an airtight container.

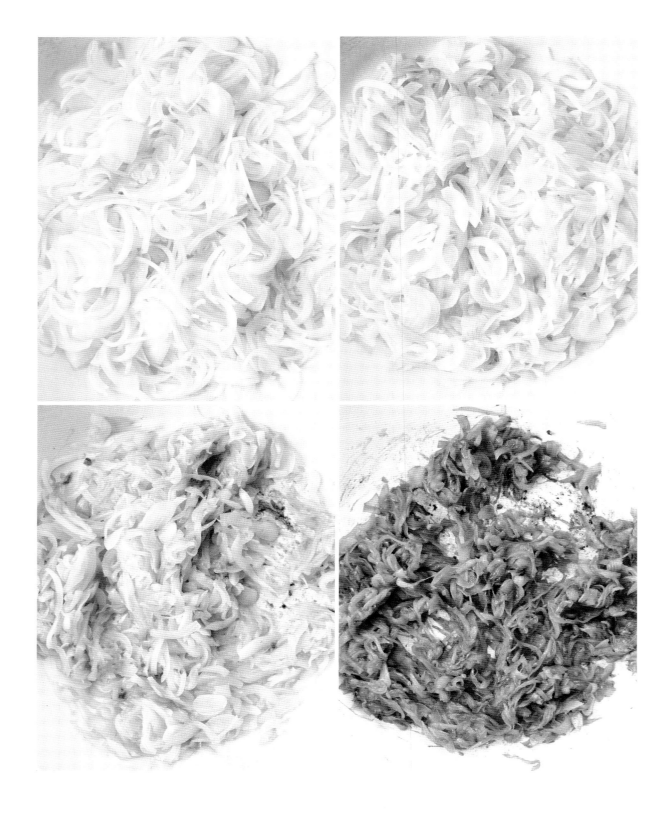

CARAMELIZED ONIONS MAKES ABOUT 2 CUPS

Many recipes call for adding a small amount of sugar when caramelizing onions, but we find that slow cooking draws out all the natural sweetness you could want, especially when you start with sweet onions. All you really need is time. The photos (opposite) show what to expect as the onions glisten, soften, brown and finally caramelize at 10, 20, 30 and 40 minutes. A jot of vinegar rounds out and deepens the onion flavor.

3 pounds sweet onions, sliced

2 tablespoons olive oil

2 fresh thyme sprigs

Kosher salt

1 tablespoon balsamic or wine vinegar, optional

COMBINE THE ONIONS, OLIVE OIL AND THYME in a large heavy skillet over moderate heat. Season with ½ teaspoon salt. Cook the mixture, stirring from time to time, until the onions are meltingly soft, browned and caramelized, 40 to 45 minutes. After about 20 minutes of cooking, you will have to stir the softened onions more often, as they begin to stick to the bottom of the pan. Make sure to scrape up that browned goodness and stir it into the onions. If you like, stir in the vinegar during the last few minutes of cooking.

DAN'S THANKSGIVING ONIONS FOR A CROWD SERVES 25 TO 30

Our friend Dan Kaplan is justly famous for his caramelized onions, which he makes in vast quantities for Thanksgiving. Because stovetop real estate is at a premium during the holidays, he moves operations outdoors, using disposable lasagna tins and a gas grill. These onions are a must on a leftover turkey sandwich. Dan sometimes substitutes cider vinegar for the balsamic and 1 cup maple syrup for the sugar—an alternative we wholeheartedly endorse.

Thinly slice **30 pounds yellow onions** then toss with **1½ cups olive or canola oil** and **½ cup kosher salt**. Divide the mixture between 2 deep disposable foil pans. Cook the onions on a gas grill over moderately low heat, stirring every half hour or so, until the onions are deeply browned, 4 to 5 hours. If too much liquid accumulates, turn up the heat and/or ladle off some of it. Mix together **1½ cups balsamic vinegar** and **¾ cup sugar** and stir into the onions. Increase the heat to moderately high and cook for another 30 minutes, stirring often to scrape up the brown bits from the sides and bottom of the pans.

ONION AND ROSEMARY FOCACCIA SERVES 8 TO 10

We spent one gray, cold and very poor winter living in Philadelphia, in a teensy apartment that looked down over an alley through which early morning garbage trucks rumbled a wake-up call. A weekly visit to Metropolitan Bakery was one of our few indulgences. Set on a picturesque corner south of Rittenhouse Square, the bakery felt so cosmopolitan, so civilized, and oh, how we looked forward to sharing a crumbly millet muffin and a giant square of perfectly oily focaccia. Funny how we look back on those months, which felt so grinding and directionless at the time, with such fondness now. That focaccia still satisfies a deep spot of hunger, and this version is easy to pull off. The addition of boiled potato yields a remarkably light and tender dough. We sometimes add a red onion to the mix, just for the splash of color.

FOR THE DOUGH

1 small russet potato

2½ cups cold water

5 cups all-purpose flour

2½ teaspoons active dry yeast

1 teaspoon sugar

Kosher salt

2 tablespoons olive oil, plus more for oiling the pan

FOR THE TOPPING

1 small sprig fresh rosemary

2 small sweet onions, thinly sliced

3 tablespoons olive oil

¾ teaspoon flaky sea salt

TO MAKE THE DOUGH, PEEL THE POTATO AND cut into 1-inch cubes. Combine the potato and 2½ cups cold water in a small saucepan, cover and bring to a boil. Boil the potato until very tender when pierced with the tip of a knife, about 15 minutes. Use a handheld blender to purée the potatoes and cooking liquid to a smooth slurry (alternately, run the mixture through a food mill or mash with a fork until as smooth as possible). Let cool until just warm (the water should not be boiling hot when added to the yeast).

Meanwhile, whisk together the flour, yeast, sugar and 1½ teaspoons salt in a large bowl. Add the olive oil and the warm potato mixture and stir until the dough just comes together (it will be very soft and sticky). Generously oil a large bowl and transfer the dough to it, rolling the dough around to coat it in the oil. Cover tightly with plastic wrap and set aside at room temperature to rise until doubled in size, about 1 hour.

Strip the rosemary leaves and coarsely chop them. Combine the rosemary, onions and olive oil in a bowl and toss together.

Heat the oven to 400°F. Lightly oil a half-sheet pan, then scrape the dough onto the pan. With lightly oiled fingers, stretch and pull the dough to fill the pan. Press your fingertips into the dough to create deep dimples. Scatter the onion mixture evenly over the dough, drizzling any remaining oil over everything. Sprinkle the sea salt over the topping. Cover the pan with a clean kitchen towel and let rise until the dough is almost level with the sides of the pan, about 1 hour.

Bake the focaccia until golden brown, 35 to 40 minutes. Remove from the oven and let cool a few minutes before cutting into big squares.

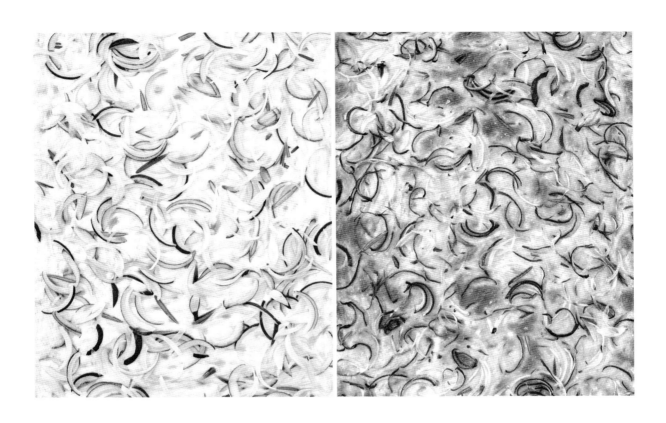

SWEET AND SALTY ONION TOASTS MAKES 24 APPETIZERS

How could we write an onion cookbook and not include James Beard's famous onion sandwiches—round tea sandwiches filled with thinly sliced onions, their edges painted with mayonnaise and rolled in chopped parsley? That's still pretty much the recipe, but when you want crunch in place of softness, these little open-faced treats are just the thing. They're delicious with an icy gin and tonic and can be made when there's almost nothing in the house but friends are at the door.

Mash together **4 tablespoons softened unsalted butter** and **1 tablespoon finely chopped parsley**. Slice **1 small sweet onion** very thinly, using a mandoline if you have one. If you don't have a sweet onion, a yellow, white or red onion works just fine—soak it in ice water for 20 minutes or so if you want to subdue the onion's bite, then drain well and pat dry. Meanwhile, cut the crusts off **12 thin slices white sandwich bread** and toast lightly. Spread the parsley butter evenly over the toasts and top with a few slices of onion, then cut each toast in half. Sprinkle a bit of **flaky sea salt** over the toasts and serve at once.

B.O.A.T. SANDWICHES MAKES 4 SANDWICHES

These sandwiches are the messy flip side to dainty Sweet and Salty Onion Toasts (page 125). You need nothing more than a big bag of chips and a cold six-pack to make this into a meal. We often switch A's—subbing avocado for arugula and adding a big forkful of Stephanie's Pickled Shallots (page 202).

1 pound bacon

2 small sweet onions, sliced

3 cups baby arugula

3 tablespoons Perfect Shallot Vinaigrette (page 199)

8 slices country bread

4 tablespoons mayonnaise

2 ripe tomatoes, cored and sliced

LAY THE BACON IN A LARGE HEAVY SKILLET, working in batches if it doesn't all fit in one go, and cook over moderate heat until crisp, about 10 minutes. Use tongs to transfer the bacon to a paper towel–lined plate to drain. Pour off all but 1 tablespoon of the fat in the skillet.

Add the onions to the fat remaining in the skillet and cook, stirring from time to time, until golden and slightly softened, 8 to 10 minutes. (We like them a little floppy but not utterly collapsed, but cook them longer if you want a more caramelized result.) Remove from the heat.

Meanwhile, toss the arugula with the vinaigrette, and toast the bread. Spread the mayonnaise over the toasted bread and layer on the bacon, onions and tomatoes. Add a pile of dressed arugula to each sandwich and top with another piece of toast. Cut each sandwich in half before diving in.

ROASTED ONIONS STUFFED WITH LENTILS, FETA AND PRUNES SERVES 4 TO 6

We love this Afghan recipe. Our vegetarian version swaps out the traditional ground lamb for lentils, and we serve it both as a main course and as part of a meze platter with hummus and a variety of salads. There is something incredibly satisfying about the way the softened onion naturally curls around the cinnamon-scented filling, sealing it in and creating a perfect torpedo-shaped package.

3 large sweet onions

2 plump garlic cloves, finely chopped

2 tablespoons olive oil, plus more for drizzling

1 teaspoon ground cumin

¼ teaspoon ground cinnamon

1½ cups cooked lentils

1 cup cooked white rice

8 prunes, chopped

½ cup finely crumbled feta

2 tablespoons finely chopped parsley, plus more for garnish

Kosher salt and freshly ground black pepper

¼ cup water

BRING A POT OF WATER TO A BOIL. AS YOU wait for the water to boil, peel the onions and trim the root end. Cut each onion lengthwise to its center—as if you were cutting the onion in half, but stopping halfway through. This will make it easier to separate the layers once the onions are boiled. Place the trimmed onions into the gently boiling water and cook until tender, about 20 minutes. Using a slotted spoon, transfer the onions to a large bowl filled with cold water. Let the onions cool in the water for a few minutes. To keep from burning your fingertips, work under the water to gently separate the softened outer layers of each onion, about 4 or 5 per onion, until you get to the stiffer middle section. Put the onion layers in a sieve to dry.

When the middle sections are cool enough to handle, remove them from the water and finely chop them (you should have about 1 cup).

Heat the oven to 375°F. Lightly oil a casserole dish. Combine the chopped onions, garlic and olive oil in a small skillet over moderate heat and cook, stirring from time to time, until softened, about 5 minutes. Stir in the cumin and cinnamon and cook for 1 minute more. Remove from the heat and scrape into a bowl. Add the lentils, rice, prunes, feta and 2 tablespoons parsley. Season with ½ teaspoon salt and several grinds of black pepper and stir everything together. Taste and adjust the seasonings.

Take 1 onion layer in the palm of your hand and fill with a heaping spoonful of stuffing. Roll the onion layer around the stuffing into a neat torpedo shape and arrange seam side down in the oiled dish. Continue with the remaining onion layers and filling, arranging them snugly in the dish. Pour ¼ cup water around the stuffed onions, then drizzle the onions with olive oil and season the tops with salt and pepper. Cover the dish with foil and bake until the onions are tender and juicy, about 45 minutes.

Remove the dish from the oven and turn on the broiler. Take off the foil and baste the onions with some of the liquid that has collected in the bottom of the dish. Broil the onions until lightly browned, a matter of a few minutes, then serve hot or at room temperature, garnished with some chopped parsley.

ZANNE'S STUFFED ONIONS SERVES 4 TO 6

The former executive food editor of *Gourmet*, Zanne Early Stewart, shared with us the outlines of a recipe that her grandmother used to make when grilling. She hollowed out onions and filled them with crumbled sausage, bread crumbs and cheese, then topped each onion with a crisscross of bacon, after which they were wrapped in foil, nestled in the coals of a charcoal grill and roasted until tender and oozy. We've taken to making these in the oven and serving them as a main course, paired with a salad—you need a little something fresh to cut all this porky richness!

6 large sweet onions

1 pound sweet or hot Italian pork sausage

1 cup fresh bread crumbs

4 slices provolone, finely chopped

¼ cup freshly grated Parmesan

2 tablespoons finely chopped flat-leaf parsley leaves

2 slices bacon, finely chopped

HEAT THE OVEN TO 400°F. SLICE OFF THE TOP quarter of the onions and discard. Peel and trim the onions. Using a sharp paring knife, core them, keeping the outer 2 to 3 layers and bottom intact. As you work, place the onions in a large gratin dish. Chop enough of the onion cores to measure about ½ cup. Discard the remaining onions cores or save for another use.

Combine the chopped onions and the sausage in a skillet and cook over moderate heat, stirring from time to time to break up the meat, until the sausage is just cooked through, 8 to 10 minutes. Scrape the sausage and onions into a bowl and let cool slightly.

Add the bread crumbs, provolone, Parmesan and parsley to the cooled sausage and stir everything together to combine, breaking up any large lumps of sausage meat.

Fill the onions with the stuffing, mounding it. Finely chop the bacon and scatter over each stuffed onion. Wrap the dish tightly in foil and bake until the onions are tender and the bacon is browned, about 1 hour. Remove the foil, baste the onions with some of the cooking juices and continue to bake until the tops are golden brown, about 10 minutes more. Serve warm.

FARRO AND VEGETABLE SALAD WITH CHARRED ONION DRESSING SERVES 6

If you invite us to a potluck, chances are this is what we'll bring. We like it because the components can be made ahead, it's perfect at room temperature, and there's something about the layers of flavors, textures and colors that pulls your fork back again and again. The beets' color will bleed once the salad is tossed, so we usually just layer the ingredients knowing that the salad will mix itself as guests reach in for a scoop.

3 beets, trimmed

3 tablespoons apple cider vinegar

7 tablespoons grapeseed oil

Kosher salt and freshly ground black pepper

2 tablespoons olive oil

2 sweet onions, halved lengthwise

½ cup farro

½ teaspoon ground cumin

4 large carrots, thickly sliced

¼ cup parsley leaves

½ teaspoon poppy seeds

3 cups baby kale or arugula

HEAT THE OVEN TO 400°F. WRAP THE BEETS in foil and roast in the oven until tender, about 1 hour. Remove from the oven and open the foil so the beets can cool slightly. When cool enough to handle, peel the beets and cut into wedges. Toss with 1 tablespoon vinegar and 1 tablespoon grapeseed oil. Season to taste with salt and pepper.

Meanwhile, heat 1 tablespoon olive oil in a heavy, oven-safe skillet over high heat. When the oil smokes, arrange the onions cut sides down in the skillet then transfer the skillet to the oven. Roast the onions until the undersides are charred and the flesh is tender, about 30 minutes.

Put the farro in a small saucepan with 1½ cups cold salted water, bring to a boil then reduce the heat and simmer until tender, 20 to 25 minutes. Drain well, then transfer to a bowl.

Heat the remaining 1 tablespoon olive oil in a medium skillet over moderately high heat. Add the cumin and cook, stirring, for 30 seconds. Add the carrots, ½ teaspoon salt and several grinds of black pepper, and cook, stirring for a few minutes until browned in spots. Add ¾ cup water, bring to a boil, then reduce the heat to moderately low and simmer until the water has evaporated and the carrots are tender, 15 to 20 minutes. Remove from the heat.

To make the dressing, place one of the charred onion halves in a blender, along with the parsley, remaining 2 tablespoons vinegar, ½ teaspoon salt and several grinds of black pepper. Blend until smooth. Add the remaining 6 tablespoons grapeseed oil and poppy seeds and pulse until well combined. Pour half of the dressing over the farro and mix well.

When the remaining charred onions are cool enough to handle, gently separate them into petals and season lightly with salt.

To assemble, arrange the beets, carrots, charred onions, farro and baby kale on a large platter or in a salad bowl. Just before serving, drizzle the remaining salad dressing over everything.

WINTER CAPRESE

SERVES 4

The colors may be all snowy whites and evergreens, but we would happily dig into this salad any day of the year. Thinly slice **1 small sweet onion** and toss with **1 teaspoon champagne or white wine vinegar, 2 tablespoons olive oil** and **salt and pepper** to taste. Tear **8 ounces fresh mozzarella** into bite-sized pieces. Gently toss the mozzarella with the onion mixture then transfer to a platter. Pit **⅓ cup green olives, such as Castelvetrano or Picholine,** and tear into pieces, scattering them over the cheese as you work. Top with a handful of **fresh parsley** and **2 tablespoons chopped toasted hazelnuts.** Sprinkle with **flaky sea salt** and serve with **crusty bread.**

BEER-BATTERED ONION RINGS SERVES 4 TO 6

Everyone's favorite guilty pleasure. After making batch after batch of onion rings (poor us!), we finally landed on this ratio, which produced the perfect combination of tender onions and crunchy coating. (It's also key to make sure your oil is the right temperature so the rings fry properly—not too fast, not too slow.) Elio and his friends like them old-school, with ketchup, but we admit to going overboard on occasion and serving these rings with a batch of Four-Onion Dip (page 153). There's no such thing as too much onion!

2 large sweet onions

2 cups buttermilk (or 1 cup plain whole-milk yogurt mixed with 1 cup water)

Kosher salt

2½ cups all-purpose flour

1 (12-ounce) bottle of beer

Peanut or vegetable oil, for frying

SLICE THE ONIONS CROSSWISE INTO ½-INCH-thick rings. Separate the rings, reserving any of the very small inner rings for another use.

Pour the buttermilk into a bowl (or whisk together the yogurt and water until smooth) and whisk in 1 teaspoon salt. Add the onion rings to the mixture and soak for 20 to 30 minutes.

While the onions soak, put 1 cup flour in a shallow baking dish. Combine the remaining 1½ cups flour in a bowl with the beer and 1½ teaspoons salt and whisk until completely smooth. The mixture should have the consistency of thin pancake batter.

Heat 2 inches of oil in a deep, heavy skillet over moderately high heat. If using a thermometer, bring the oil to about 375°F. Line a baking sheet with newspapers or paper towels and set up near the skillet.

Using tongs or a slotted spoon, gather up 6 to 8 onion rings from the buttermilk, letting the excess drip back into the bowl, and drop into the flour. Toss until lightly coated then dip the rings into the beer batter, letting the excess batter drip off. Carefully slip the rings into the hot oil and fry, flipping once, until golden and crisp, about 2 minutes per batch. Transfer the rings to the lined baking sheet and season with salt. Skim out any small pieces of onion or batter left behind that can begin to burn. Continue coating and frying the remaining onions until done.

SKINNY RINGS SERVES 4

These crisp, salty threads are delicious with a squeeze of lemon—like vegetarian fried calamari—or piled high on a cheeseburger or grilled steak. Scatter any leftovers over mac and cheese before baking. They keep well and will stay crisp for several hours, so you can fry them ahead of time—but they're a dangerous proposition to have hanging around, especially if cold beers are also in the picture.

1 large sweet onion

1 cup buttermilk (or 1 cup plain whole-milk yogurt mixed with 1 cup water)

Kosher salt

1 cup all-purpose flour

½ cup fine cornmeal

1 teaspoon Aleppo pepper

½ teaspoon paprika

Freshly ground black pepper

Peanut or vegetable oil, for frying

Lemon wedges, for serving

SLICE THE ONION AS THINLY AS POSSIBLE, preferably using a mandoline. Combine the buttermilk and 1 teaspoon salt in a bowl and whisk together until the salt is dissolved. Add the onion rings to the buttermilk and let soak for 20 minutes.

Meanwhile, whisk together the flour, cornmeal, Aleppo pepper, paprika, 1 teaspoon salt and several grinds of black pepper in a shallow dish.

Heat 1 inch of oil in large heavy skillet over moderately high heat. If using a thermometer, bring the oil to about 375°F. Line a baking sheet with newspapers or paper towels and set up near the skillet.

Using tongs, gather up about ¼ cup onions from the buttermilk, letting the excess drip back into the bowl. Drop the onions into the seasoned flour and toss until lightly coated, shaking off any excess and gently separating the rings so they don't clump together too much. Carefully slip the rings into the hot oil and fry, flipping once with a slotted spoon, until golden and crisp, 60 to 90 seconds per batch. Remove the onions, letting the excess oil drip back into the skillet, and transfer to the lined baking sheet to drain. Skim out any small pieces of onion or breading that are left behind and can begin to burn. Continue coating and frying the remaining onions until done. Serve the fried onions warm or at room temperature with lemon wedges on the side.

ZA'ATAR ONION PETALS WITH BEETS AND LABNEH SERVES 6

Chef Josh Thomsen introduced us to a dish of crisp fried onion wedges that were the perfect size and shape for scooping up a vivid dip of minced roasted beets. We also love the fried chicken dusted with za'atar—a popular Middle Eastern seasoning blend of sesame seeds, sumac and thyme—served at Federal Donuts in Philadelphia. And so a mashup was born: fried onion petals seasoned with za'atar and meant to be dipped in a lemony mash of beets and labneh. Ketchup who?

1 large beet

2 teaspoons freshly squeezed lemon juice

Kosher salt and freshly ground black pepper

2 large sweet onions

2 cups buttermilk (or 1 cup plain whole-milk yogurt mixed with 1 cup water)

3 cups rice flour

1 teaspoon salt

2½ cups club soda

Peanut or vegetable oil, for frying

1 cup labneh or Greek yogurt

Fresh mint leaves

1 tablespoon za'atar

HEAT THE OVEN TO 400°F. WRAP THE BEET tightly in aluminum foil and roast until tender, about 45 minutes. Remove from the oven and loosen the foil. When the beet is cool enough to handle, peel and cut it into a few large chunks. Place in a food processor and pulse a few times until finely chopped, but not juiced. Transfer the chopped beet to a bowl and stir in the lemon juice. Season with salt and several grinds of black pepper. Refrigerate until ready to serve.

Cut each onion lengthwise into 8 wedges. Separate the wedges into "petals"—use only the outermost wedges, saving the smaller inner pieces for another use. Pour the buttermilk into a large bowl and add the onions, setting aside to soak for an hour or so.

Put 1½ cups rice flour in a medium bowl and whisk in 1 teaspoon salt. Whisk in the club soda until smooth. Put the remaining 1½ cups rice flour in a shallow dish.

When ready to fry, heat about 2 inches of oil in a deep heavy skillet over moderately high heat. If using a thermometer, bring the oil to about 375°F. Line a baking sheet with newspapers or paper towels.

Scoop up a few of the onion petals from the buttermilk, letting the excess drip back into the bowl, then dredge in the rice flour until lightly coated, before dipping in the batter. Add the battered petals to the hot oil and fry, flipping once, until golden brown all over, 2 to 3 minutes per batch. Transfer the petals to the lined baking sheet and repeat with the remaining onions, allowing the oil to come back to temperature between batches. Keep the onions warm in a very low oven until ready to serve.

Spoon the labneh into a small bowl and top with the beet mixture. Mince a few mint leaves and scatter over the beets. Transfer the onion petals to a platter and sprinkle with the za'atar and some salt. Serve with the beet and yogurt mixture.

NOTE: The combination of rice flour and club soda makes for a very light crispy crust. You can use this same batter for making regular onion rings, instead of the Beer-Battered Onion Rings (page 137).

ONION TACOS MAKES 12 TACOS

We once ate the most delicious onion tacos at a swanky taco joint in Pittsburgh. They were simplicity itself—juicy rings of softly cooked onions folded into warm tortillas. There must have been more to them, but that was the takeaway. As time went on, those tacos became legendary in our minds. Were they really as good as we remembered? We'll never know, since the place is long closed. But then we made these, and they are even better.

Make the **Grilled Onion Rings,** following the recipe below. Transfer them to a plate and cover to keep warm. Lay **12 good-quality corn tortillas** (double this amount if your tortillas are very thin) over the grill and toast, turning once, until softened and blackened in spots, about 3 minutes total. Wrap the tortillas in a clean kitchen towel to steam and keep warm. To assemble the tacos, slide the onions off the skewers. Fill each tortilla with a few onion rings, top with a spoonful of **Roasted Tomatillo Salsa** (page 296) or **Fresh Tomatillo Salsa** (page 296) and a generous scattering of **crumbled queso fresco**.

GRILLED ONION RINGS SERVES 4 TO 6

We always make room on the grill for these skewered onions—they make the perfect topping for grilled sausages, burgers, steak, fish, even hot dogs. Or, coarsely chop the rings and add them to a salad.

If using bamboo skewers, soak them in water for at least 30 minutes before grilling. Preheat a grill over moderately high heat (alternately, you can use a stovetop grill pan).

Cut **4 sweet onions** crosswise into ½-inch-thick slices. Keeping the sliced rings intact, thread them onto the skewers. Stir together **2 tablespoons olive oil,** ½ **teaspoon oregano,** ½ **teaspoon salt** and **several grinds of black pepper** in a small bowl. Brush the mixture over the skewered onions.

Grill until softened and charred in spots, flipping occasionally, 10 to 12 minutes. Remove the onions from the skewers and serve warm.

SWEET ONION AND APPLE JAM MAKES ABOUT 4 HALF-PINTS

Onions, hot pepper and a double dose of apples—fresh fruit and cider vinegar—come together in a spiced jam that's pretty perfect on a toasted everything bagel with cream cheese. It also shines on meat—try it as a glaze for pork or chicken, like the Sticky Jammy Chicken Wings (below). The jam will keep for months on a cool, dark shelf in the pantry.

2 medium sweet onions

1 Granny Smith apple

½ cup apple cider vinegar

1½ cups sugar

Freshly grated zest of 1 lemon

½ teaspoon crushed red pepper flakes

2 tablespoons powdered pectin

STERILIZE 4 HALF-PINT JARS (OR TWICE THAT many 4-ounce jars); we like to do this by setting the jars in a roasting pan and heating them in a 225°F oven for 20 minutes; then turn off the oven and leave the jars inside until you are ready to fill them.

Coarsely chop the onions; you should have about 3 cups chopped onions. Leaving its skin on, core the apple and chop it. Working in batches if necessary, purée the onions and apple with the vinegar in a blender until very smooth.

Transfer the vinegar and onion slurry to a heavy pot and stir in the sugar, lemon zest and red pepper flakes. Bring the mixture to a boil over moderately high heat, skimming the foam that rises to the top (doing so will result in a nice clear jam). When the mixture has boiled for 5 minutes, increase the heat to high, stir in the pectin and boil hard for 1 minute more. Remove from the heat and transfer the jam to the sterilized jars, leaving ½ inch of space at the top. Seal the jars, immediately turn upside down and let cool. If one jar cannot be filled completely, refrigerate it and use it first.

STICKY JAMMY CHICKEN WINGS SERVES 4 TO 6

It's not a crime to lick your fingers! Heat the oven to 400°F. Line 2 baking sheets with foil (this will make cleanup easier) and set a wire rack inside of each. Place **5 pounds chicken wings** in a large bowl, add **3 tablespoons olive oil, 1 tablespoon kosher salt** and **several grinds of black pepper** and toss to coat. Spread the wings in a single layer on the prepared racks. Bake the wings until they are cooked through and the skin is crispy, about 45 minutes. Using tongs, transfer the wings to the cleaned bowl, add **1½ cups Sweet Onion and Apple Jam** and toss to coat. Return the wings to the racks and bake until glazed and very well browned in spots, about 10 minutes. Serve at once, with plenty of napkins.

THE LEAN GREENS
SCALLIONS & CHIVES

Scallions. Sometimes called green onions or Welsh onions, scallions are the most common fresh onion and are available in the supermarket year round. They are an inexpensive treat, and we always make sure to grab a bunch or two. These slender, tender alliums can be used both raw and cooked, and one of their great benefits is that they don't cause tears the way other onions do. Scallions usually have white-skinned bulbs, but yellow- and red-skinned scallions are also available, though more often from a local farmer than the grocery store. Unless stated otherwise, when we call for scallions in a recipe, we mean the whole thing, from the rounded white bulb to the hollow green leaves, trimmed only of the wispy roots and any ragged or wilted greens. Stored in a plastic bag in the fridge, scallions will last at least a week.

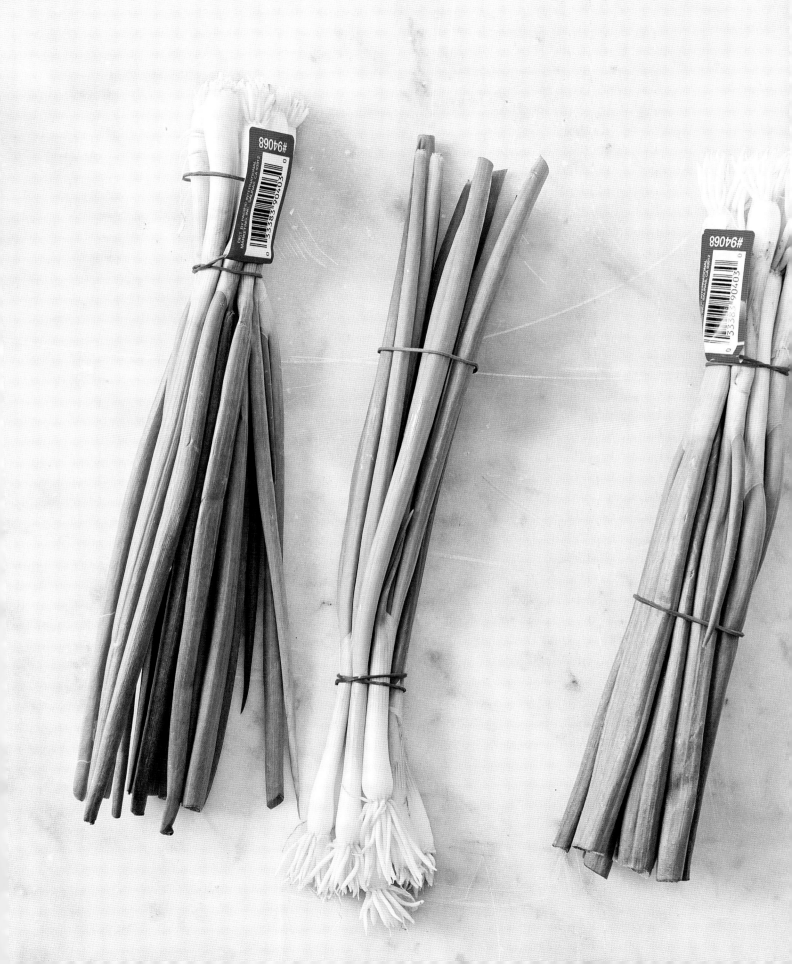

GRITS WITH SCALLIONS AND BACON SERVES 4 TO 6

Sunday morning, a fresh foot of snow on the walk—this recipe, inspired by one from chef Edna Lewis, is exactly what you want to eat when you come inside from shoveling. And who would say no to a poached egg on top?

5 cups water

1 cup stoneground grits

Kosher salt

4 ounces smoked bacon

5 bunches scallions

1 plump garlic clove, finely chopped

Freshly ground black pepper

1 cup heavy cream

Whole nutmeg

BRING THE WATER TO A BOIL IN A HEAVY saucepan then reduce the heat to moderate, so that it simmers gently. Add the grits in a slow stream, whisking constantly to keep lumps from forming. Continue whisking for about 3 minutes after all the grits have been added, then reduce the heat to low and cook, stirring regularly to keep from scorching, until the grits are creamy and fully tender, 30 to 40 minutes. Cover and keep warm over very low heat until ready to serve.

Meanwhile, cook the bacon in a heavy skillet over moderately high heat until crisp, 7 to 8 minutes. While the bacon cooks, trim the scallions and slice them into ½-inch pieces. When the bacon is ready, transfer it to a paper towel-lined plate to cool. Add the scallions and garlic to the bacon fat in the skillet and cook over moderately high heat until crisp-tender, about 5 minutes. Season with ½ teaspoon salt and plenty of freshly ground black pepper. Add the cream, reduce the heat, and simmer until slightly thickened, 4 to 5 minutes. Grate a little nutmeg over the scallion mixture.

To serve, spoon the grits into warm bowls and top with plenty of the creamed scallions. Crumble the bacon over each bowl and serve at once.

FOUR-ONION DIP MAKES ABOUT 2 CUPS

You might argue that onion dip could appear almost anywhere in this book, but the scallions—their color and fresh bite—are what really bring this version to life. We have made this successfully with red, yellow and sweet onions, so feel free to use whatever you have on hand.

2 onions, finely chopped

2 plump garlic cloves, finely chopped

2 tablespoons olive oil

Kosher salt and freshly ground black pepper

3 scallions, finely chopped

1 cup sour cream

1 teaspoon freshly squeezed lemon juice, plus more to taste

1 teaspoon Worcestershire sauce

1 tablespoon finely chopped chives, for garnish

COMBINE THE ONIONS, GARLIC AND OLIVE oil in a medium skillet over moderately high heat. Season with salt and plenty of black pepper and cook, stirring from time to time, until golden, about 10 minutes. Scrape into a bowl to cool.

Add the scallions, sour cream, lemon juice and Worcestershire sauce to the onions. Season the dip with plenty of black pepper and mix well. Taste and adjust the seasonings, adding more lemon juice to taste. Go easy on adding more salt since you will likely be using this dip with salty potato chips.

Transfer the dip to a serving bowl and top with the chives.

OLIVE DIP MAKES ABOUT 1½ CUPS

A classic in Kate's family—always served with pre-dinner drinks—this is one of the first recipes she learned to make as a child. Finely chop **1 bunch scallions** and mash into **1 (8-ounce) block of softened cream cheese**. Finely chop **1 cup drained pimiento-stuffed green olives** (nothing fancy, please!) and mash into the cream cheese, adding a little olive juice from the jar for extra flavor if you like. Serve with carrot sticks and crackers, preferably Triscuits or Ritz.

SCALLION NIGELLA FLATBREADS MAKES 10 FLATBREADS

Nigella seeds, sometimes labeled as kalonji or black onion seeds, are small, triangular ebony seeds that offer up a peppery bite. They are used often in Indian and Middle Eastern cooking, and here add a bit of crunch and an extra layer of flavor to the naan-like flatbreads. Look for them in natural foods or specialty markets. We love filling these breads with rosy slices of lamb and some Tomato, Cucumber and Red Onion Salad (page 95), but they're also delicious as an appetizer with Mint Raita (page 45).

1 teaspoon honey

¾ cup warm water

2¼ teaspoons active dry yeast

4 cups all-purpose flour, plus more if needed

½ cup plain whole-milk yogurt

2 tablespoons vegetable oil

Kosher salt

6 scallions, finely chopped

1 tablespoon nigella seeds

COMBINE THE HONEY AND WARM WATER IN a large bowl and stir until the honey is dissolved. Stir in the yeast then let sit until the mixture is foamy, about 10 minutes.

Stir the flour, yogurt, vegetable oil and ½ teaspoon salt into the yeast mixture. Add the scallions and knead the dough in the bowl (or turn out onto a lightly floured surface) by hand until smooth, about 5 minutes, adding a little more flour if the dough is sticky. Shape the dough into a ball, cover the bowl with a clean kitchen towel and let sit in a warm place to rise until doubled in size, about 1 hour.

Using a sharp knife, divide the dough into 10 pieces and shape into balls. Heat a cast-iron or other heavy nonstick skillet over moderately high heat. Working with 1 piece at a time, roll the dough out with a rolling pin so that it's about ¼ inch thick. Sprinkle some nigella seeds over one side of the dough and press gently to adhere. Lay the dough seed side up in the dry, hot skillet and cook until the underside is lightly blistered and the bread is puffed, about 2 minutes. Flip the flatbread and continue to cook until the second side is blistered and the flatbread is cooked through, 1 to 2 minutes more. Remove the flatbread from the skillet and wrap in foil or a clean kitchen towel to keep warm until ready to serve.

As one flatbread cooks, roll out the next piece of dough so that it is ready to go into the skillet as soon as one comes out. Continue with the remaining pieces of dough.

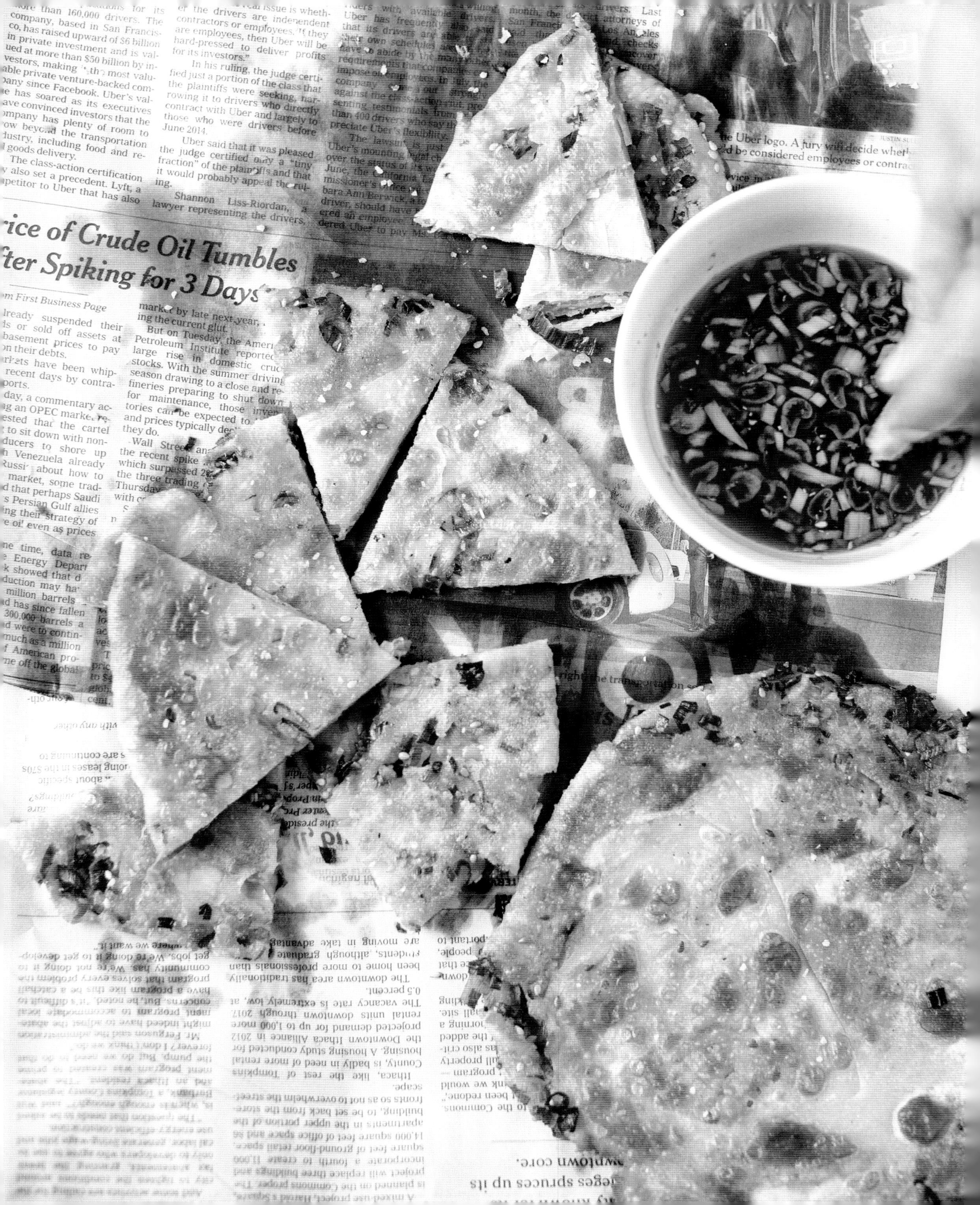
rice of Crude Oil Tumbles
fter Spiking for 3 Days

SCALLION SESAME PANCAKES MAKES 6 PANCAKES

Crisp, chewy, deliciously greasy—scallion pancakes are fun to eat, but they're good fun to make as well. The technique of brushing the dough with sesame oil then rolling it into a spiral and rolling it flat again is a form of lamination—similar to what happens when you add sheets of butter to dough when making croissants, with the effect of creating flaky layers. Making scallion pancakes sounds more complicated than it actually is, but after making one or two, you'll feel like a pro.

FOR THE PANCAKES

3 cups all-purpose flour, plus extra for dusting

Kosher salt

1½ cups boiling water

4 bunches scallions

3 tablespoons toasted sesame oil, or as needed

1 tablespoon sesame seeds

Peanut or vegetable oil, for frying

FOR THE DIPPING SAUCE

2 tablespoons vinegar from Chinese Pickled Garlic (page 295) or black vinegar

2 tablespoons soy sauce

1 teaspoon sugar

1 clove Chinese Pickled Garlic (page 295) or 1 plump garlic clove, finely chopped

TO MAKE THE PANCAKES, PLACE THE FLOUR and ½ teaspoon salt in the bowl of a food processor; pulse a few times to combine. With the processor running, drizzle in about 1¼ cups of the boiling water, then continue to process for about 10 seconds more. If the dough has not come together, drizzle in more water, 1 tablespoon at a time, until it does. Transfer the dough to a lightly floured work surface and knead a few times to form a smooth ball. Transfer to a bowl, cover with a clean, damp kitchen towel and let rest at room temperature for at least 30 minutes, or while you prepare the remaining ingredients. The dough may be refrigerated overnight.

Trim off the white part of each scallion and reserve for another use. Slice the scallion greens very thinly. Measure out 1 tablespoon of the scallion greens to use in the dipping sauce and set the remainder aside. You should have about 2 cups.

To make the dipping sauce, combine the vinegar, soy sauce and sugar, stirring until the sugar is dissolved. Stir in the pickled garlic. Sprinkle the scallion greens over the sauce and set aside.

To shape the pancakes, divide the dough into 6 even pieces and roll each between the palms of your hands into a smooth ball. Working with 1 ball of dough at a time (loosely cover the remaining dough with the damp towel), roll it out with a

CONTINUED

rolling pin on a lightly floured work surface into an 8-inch disc (1). Using a pastry brush, brush a thin layer of sesame oil over the top of the dough (2). Roll the dough up like a jelly roll (3), then tightly roll it again like a snail's shell, tucking the end underneath (4). Set the roll down on the work surface, spiral side up, and flatten gently with your hand (5). Re-roll the dough into an 8-inch disc (6).

Brush the top of the dough with another thin layer of sesame oil. Sprinkle about ⅓ cup scallions and ½ teaspoon sesame seeds evenly over the dough (7). Roll up again like a jelly roll (8) and twist again into a tight spiral, tucking the end underneath. Flatten the spiral gently and roll into a 7-inch disc (9).

Repeat these steps with the remaining balls of dough, sesame oil, scallions and sesame seeds. (Once you get good at shaping the pancakes, you might find it easier and faster to start cooking 1 pancake while shaping the next, so it is ready to slide into the oil as the first comes out.)

Line a large plate with newspaper or clean paper bags. Heat about ¼ inch oil in a medium cast-iron or nonstick skillet over moderately high heat. When the oil shimmers, carefully slip 1 pancake into it. Cook, shaking the pan gently from time to time, until the underside is golden brown, 1½ to 2 minutes. Using tongs, carefully flip the pancake and continue to cook, again shaking the pan gently as needed, until the second side is golden brown, 1½ to 2 minutes more. Transfer to the lined plate to drain. Sprinkle the pancake with a pinch of salt and cut into 6 wedges. Serve immediately with the sauce for dipping, while you cook the remaining pancakes in the same manner, adding a little more oil to the skillet as needed.

KIMCHI SCALLION OMELET SERVES 2 TO 4

We adore kimchi: on rice, straight out of the jar, however we can get it. This thin omelet has so much flavor all on its own that it usually doesn't need a sauce. But to go the extra mile, we sometimes stir up a little bowl of 3 tablespoons soy sauce and 2 teaspoons rice vinegar, then add a few matchsticks of fresh ginger and thinly sliced scallion greens. This omelet makes a great accompaniment to Kalbi (page 164) or Warm Tofu with Spicy Scallion Sauce (page 167).

½ cup all-purpose flour

Kosher salt and freshly ground black pepper

¼ cup water

2 large eggs

3 scallions

2 tablespoons vegetable oil

1 cup Easiest Kimchi (page 163), coarsely chopped

WHISK TOGETHER THE FLOUR, ¼ TEASPOON salt and several grinds of black pepper in a bowl. Measure the water into a liquid measuring cup, then crack the eggs into the water and whisk together. Pour the egg mixture over the flour and whisk until very smooth. Quarter the scallions lengthwise then cut crosswise into 2-inch lengths.

Heat the vegetable oil in a medium nonstick skillet over moderately high heat, swirling to coat the bottom of the pan. Lay the scallion pieces evenly over the bottom of the skillet, followed by the chopped kimchi. Give the batter another thorough whisking and pour over the scallions and kimchi, tilting the pan to make sure everything is covered evenly. Cook, undisturbed, until the underside is golden brown and set, about 3 minutes. Loosen with a rubber spatula and flip the omelet. Continue cooking until the omelet is completely set, about 2 minutes more.

Slide onto a plate or cutting board and cut into wedges before digging in.

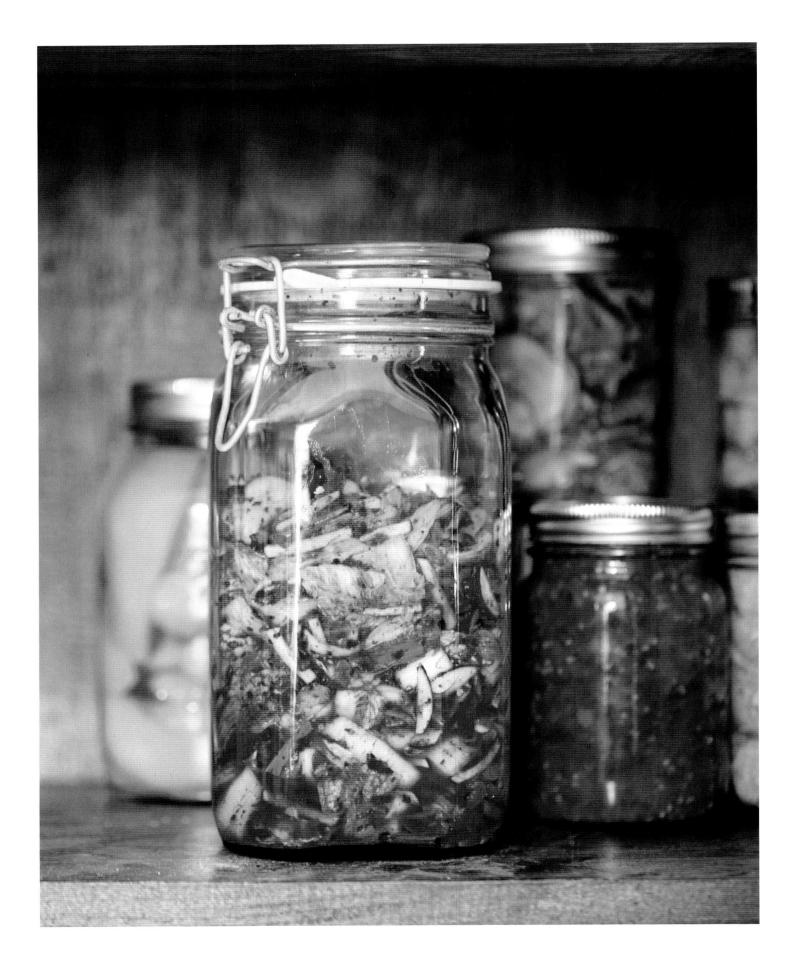

EASIEST KIMCHI MAKES ABOUT 6 CUPS

Like Pickled Red Onions (page 104), there is always a jar of homemade kimchi in our fridge. The fermented mix of cabbage, scallions and Korean red chile flakes spices up everything it touches—we add it to our morning eggs, stir it into leftover rice for an easy lunch or serve it over grilled steak. Fish sauce adds a little extra funk, but it can be omitted if you want to keep this kimchi vegetarian. We've also made it successfully with red radishes in place of the daikon.

3 pounds napa cabbage
(about 1 very large head)

Kosher salt

6 plump garlic cloves, finely grated

2-inch piece fresh ginger, finely grated

1½ teaspoons sugar

¼ cup gochugaru (Korean red chile flakes)

2 teaspoons fish sauce, optional

12 ounces daikon, peeled and cut into matchsticks

1 bunch scallions, trimmed and cut into 1-inch pieces

CUT THE CABBAGE LENGTHWISE INTO quarters and remove the cores. Cut each quarter crosswise into 2-inch-wide strips. Place the cabbage in a very large bowl and sprinkle 6 tablespoons salt over it. Scrunch the cabbage with your hands until it starts to soften and release its water. Put a plate on top on top of the cabbage and weigh it down with something heavy, like a jar or can of beans. Let the cabbage sit for 2 hours (it will release lots of water as it sits).

While the cabbage sits, combine the garlic, ginger, sugar, gochugaru and fish sauce, if using, in a small bowl and stir until well combined. The mixture will become a thick paste. Set aside.

Drain and rinse the cabbage well under cold running water, then drain in a colander. Wash the bowl the cabbage soaked in.

Using your hands, squeeze as much remaining water from the cabbage as possible and return it to the cleaned bowl. Add the daikon, scallions and chile paste. Mix everything thoroughly using your hands (if you like, wear disposable gloves to protect yourself from the chile). Gently work the paste into the vegetables until they are evenly coated. Tightly pack the kimchi into 3 clean wide-mouth glass pint jars (or a variety of smaller jars), pressing down until brine rises to cover the vegetables. Fill three small resealable plastic bags with water, seal and set on top of the vegetables to help submerge them in the brine. Set the jars on a tray to catch any overflowing liquid.

Set aside in a cool room temperature place for 5 days. Check the kimchi once a day, pressing down on the vegetables with a spoon to keep them submerged under the brine. You may see bubbles inside the jar and brine may seep out from beneath the plastic bag filled with water.

After 5 days, taste the kimchi. If it's ripe enough for your liking, seal the jar and transfer it to the refrigerator. You may eat it right away, but the flavor will continue to improve if you can wait a few more days.

KALBI SERVES 6

Years ago, our friends Franky and Jenni shared their recipe for Korean beef ribs, cheekily illustrated by Franky with a black and white watercolor. Pulling out the piece of art when we're ready to make the recipe always makes us smile, and the ribs themselves are so crazy good that as soon as we eat the last one we start planning when to make them again. Though they need to marinate overnight, these are a snap to pull together and deliver such huge flavor—perfect for a party where no one cares if they get a little messy. Talk with your butcher before ordering the meat, making sure to specify flanken-style short ribs, in which the meat is cut across the bones, rather than between the ribs. They should be sliced quite thinly, about ⅜ inch thick. We like to serve kalbi with steamed white rice and a bowl of Easiest Kimchi (page 163) or Scallion and Cilantro Chimichurri (page 263).

6 scallions, chopped

6 plump garlic cloves, chopped

½ cup soy sauce

⅓ cup toasted sesame oil

⅓ cup sugar

5 pounds thinly sliced flanken short ribs

COMBINE THE SCALLIONS, GARLIC, SOY sauce, sesame oil and sugar in a bowl, stirring until the sugar dissolves. Pour the marinade into a very large resealable plastic bag. Add the ribs, stir to coat, squeeze all the air from the bag and seal. Marinate in the refrigerator overnight.

Preheat a grill over high heat. Remove the ribs from the marinade and grill, flipping them halfway through, until sizzling and charred in spots, about 8 minutes. Remove from the heat and serve at once (though a leftover cold rib for breakfast is mighty fine, too).

WARM TOFU WITH SPICY SCALLION SAUCE SERVES 4

Kate first tasted this dish while working on a Korean menu at *Gourmet*. The recipe quickly went into regular rotation because our then-two-year-old son loved it as much as we did (plus, it only takes minutes to assemble). It's normally served as a *banchan*, one of the numerous small savory and spicy dishes that accompany a Korean meal, but we usually make it the star of a weeknight supper, paired with steamed broccoli and rice.

1 (16-ounce) package **firm tofu**

1 plump **garlic clove**

Kosher salt

2 teaspoons **sesame seeds**

4 **scallions**, finely chopped

3 tablespoons **soy sauce**

1 tablespoon **toasted sesame oil**

1 teaspoon **gochugaru**
(**Korean red chile flakes**)

½ teaspoon **sugar**

RINSE THE TOFU, THEN COVER WITH COLD water in a medium saucepan. Bring to a simmer over moderately high heat, then keep warm, covered, over very low heat.

Meanwhile, mince the garlic then mash to a paste with a pinch of salt. Transfer the garlic paste to a small bowl. Toast the sesame seeds in a small skillet over moderate heat, swirling to keep the seeds from burning, until fragrant and nutty, about 2 minutes. Scrape the sesame seeds into the bowl, and add the scallions, soy sauce, sesame oil, gochugaru and sugar. Stir together until the sugar is dissolved.

Just before serving, lift the tofu from the saucepan with a large spatula and drain on paper towels. Gently pat dry, then transfer to a shallow bowl. Spoon some of the sauce over the block of tofu and serve warm with steamed rice and the remaining sauce on the side.

CHAMP
SCALLION MASHED POTATOES SERVES 6

These traditional Irish mashed potatoes, threaded through with plenty of scallions, are meant to be served with a lake of butter on top. We also like the Canal House trick of slipping smaller pats of butter throughout the potatoes (sneak them in as you spoon the spuds into a serving dish)—who wouldn't want to happen upon such a buttery pocket? Leftovers make a delicious topping for Tuesday's Shepherd's Pie (page 67).

3 pounds Yukon gold potatoes, peeled and quartered

Kosher salt

1½ cups whole milk

2 bunches scallions, finely chopped

6 tablespoons salted butter, preferably Irish

PUT THE POTATOES IN A HEAVY POT FILLED with cold water and season liberally with salt. Bring to a boil then reduce the heat to moderate and simmer, uncovered, until the potatoes are soft, about 20 minutes.

While the potatoes cook, heat the milk in a small saucepan over moderately high heat until it just comes to a simmer. Turn off the heat under the saucepan and add the scallions to the milk.

Drain the potatoes well then return them to the pot and place over low heat. Warm the potatoes for a couple of minutes, occasionally shaking the pot. This will help dry out the potatoes, making a fluffier mash. Using a potato masher, mash the potatoes until almost smooth. Cut 4 tablespoons butter into the potatoes, pour in the milk and scallions and season with 1 teaspoon salt. Continue to mash until the potatoes are smooth. Transfer to a warmed serving bowl, make a wide depression in the center and nestle the remaining 2 tablespoons butter in the hollow. Serve at once.

SCALLION MISO BUTTER

MAKES ABOUT ½ CUP

Our favorite topper for baked sweet
potatoes, this easy compound butter
is also good on Salt-Baked Sweet
Onions (page 116) or stirred into
steamed rice. Simply mash together
6 tablespoons softened butter,
1 tablespoon white miso and
4 finely chopped scallions. Place
in a ramekin or shape into a log and
wrap well in wax paper. It will keep
for a week or two in the fridge.

SCALLION TABBOULEH SERVES 6 TO 8

Another staple in our house, this bulgur salad goes with everything from Lentil Salad 101 (page 96) to Chicken and Chickpeas with Preserved Lemon Relish (page 110) or Grilled Lamb Chops Two Ways (page 304). Sometimes we substitute quinoa for the bulgur, taking extra time to cool and dry the quinoa to give it plenty of fluff.

2 cups coarse bulgur

1½ cups boiling water

2 bunches scallions, finely chopped

1 large bunch flat-leaf parsley, finely chopped

1 large bunch mint, finely chopped

Freshly grated zest and juice of 1 lemon

2 tablespoons olive oil

2 teaspoons ground sumac

Kosher salt and freshly ground pepper

PUT THE BULGUR IN A BOWL THEN POUR 1½ cups boiling water over it. Cover the bowl and let it sit for about 20 minutes; the bulgur should absorb all the water and become chewy-tender. If any water remains in the bowl, drain it. Spread the bulgur out on a large platter to dry and cool, giving it a stir every so often.

Transfer the cooled bulgur to a bowl and add the chopped scallions, parsley, mint, lemon zest and juice, olive oil, sumac, 1 teaspoon salt and a few grinds of black pepper. Stir everything together. Taste and adjust the seasonings to your liking, adding a little more lemon juice, olive oil, salt or sumac as needed. (Guy likes his salad more oily, while Kate prefers it drier and fluffier—to each their own.)

GREEN GAZPACHO WITH ALMONDS SERVES 4

We have learned so much about good food over the years from Guy's sister Christine, one of the best cooks we know. This jade-green gazpacho exemplifies her style of cooking: healthy, beautiful, surprising, satisfying. She likes to garnish it with a swirl of plain yogurt, but we love the added crunch that comes from the fried nuts.

4 scallions, coarsely chopped

1 green bell pepper, coarsely chopped

1 medium cucumber, peeled, seeded and coarsely chopped

½ to 1 jalapeño, chopped

1 plump garlic clove, chopped

1 cup water

¾ teaspoon ground cumin

Kosher salt

3 cups spinach leaves

½ cup cilantro

4 tablespoons olive oil

2 tablespoons sherry vinegar

⅓ cup almonds, coarsely chopped

COMBINE THE SCALLIONS, BELL PEPPER, cucumber, jalapeño, garlic, water, ½ teaspoon cumin and ½ teaspoon salt in a blender. Pulse until the ingredients are almost smooth.

Add the spinach, cilantro, 2 tablespoons olive oil and the vinegar. Blend until the mixture is very smooth, adding a drop or two of water if necessary to thin the soup. Taste and adjust the seasonings. Refrigerate until very cold.

Heat the remaining 2 tablespoons olive oil in a small skillet over moderate heat. Add the almonds and the remaining ¼ teaspoon cumin and fry, stirring frequently, until almonds are golden brown and nutty smelling, 3 to 5 minutes. Using a slotted spoon, transfer the nuts to a paper towel–lined plate to cool; season with salt.

Serve the gazpacho garnished with some of the fried almonds.

CONGEE SERVES 4 TO 6

When we lived on Bleecker Street in Manhattan, many nights we made our way south, on foot or by subway, to Chinatown, seeking out bowls of steaming, comforting congee—rice simmered in a great deal of liquid until it breaks down into a delicious mush of a soup. At Great New York Noodletown, the rice soup often came topped with shards of the crackling roast duck that decorated the restaurant's front windows. At Congee Village on Bowery, a few slivered scallions sufficed. Now, bereft of a local Chinatown and left to our own devices, we make congee ourselves and usually keep it vegetarian. (If you happen to be soaking any dried mushrooms, the leftover soaking liquid makes a great addition.) We top it simply with a drizzle of soy sauce, a splash of sesame oil and sprinkle of scallion greens.

6 scallions, coarsely chopped

5 plump garlic cloves, smashed

2-inch piece of fresh ginger, thinly sliced

1 cup Arborio or sushi rice

9 cups water or chicken broth

Kosher salt

Soy sauce, toasted sesame oil and chopped scallion greens, for serving

PLACE A LARGE SQUARE OF CHEESECLOTH on the counter and lay the scallions, garlic and ginger in the center. Tie up the corners of the cheesecloth like a hobo's bundle and drop into a large heavy pot. Add the rice, water and 1 teaspoon salt. Bring to a boil over high heat then reduce the heat to low and simmer gently, uncovered, until the rice is very tender and falling apart and the mixture is soupy, 1 to 1½ hours. Remove the cheesecloth bundle, pressing on it to extract some of the liquid, and discard. Serve the congee in warm bowls, topped with a drizzle of soy sauce and sesame oil and a scattering of scallion greens.

NOTE: Any leftovers kept in the fridge will soak up all the surrounding liquid. When you reheat the congee, simply add more water to thin it out (and maybe a pinch of salt). Like your favorite grandmother, congee is infinitely forgiving.

CREAMY CHIVE DRESSING MAKES ABOUT 1½ CUPS

We turn to this classic recipe from chef and cookbook author Patricia Wells when the chives are really coming up in the garden. Drizzle it over a sturdy salad of endive and fennel or a platter of sliced tomatoes (a little bacon wouldn't hurt!). This recipe makes enough to dress 2 pounds small boiled potatoes, transforming them into the simplest, most delicious potato salad.

Combine **1 teaspoon finely grated lemon zest, 2 tablespoons freshly squeezed lemon juice, ½ teaspoon salt** and **several grinds of black pepper** in a pint jar, seal and shake well until the salt is dissolved. Add **1 cup half-and-half** and **½ cup finely chopped chives** and shake until well combined and slightly thickened. Taste and adjust the seasoning. Refrigerate until ready to use, up to three days. Give it a good shake before using.

BLUE CHEESE AND CHIVE DRESSING

Lemon and half-and-half react together in a way that mimics the flavor and voluptuousness of buttermilk. We sometimes add ½ cup finely crumbled blue cheese to the recipe above for a very fast version of the beloved tangy dressing.
—MAKES ABOUT 2 CUPS

FINES HERBES DRESSING

Fines herbes is a classic French combination of tender herbs—usually tarragon, parsley, chervil and chives in equal measure—that is especially nice in vinaigrettes, sprinkled over vegetables and folded into omelets. Simply replace all of the chives in Creamy Chive Dressing with ½ cup fines herbes (about 2 tablespoons each of finely chopped tarragon, parsley, chervil and chives).
—MAKES ABOUT 1½ CUPS

CHIVE PASTA WITH SIX-ALLIUM SAUCE SERVES 4 TO 6

One of the many things Guy brought to our relationship was his sturdy, hand-crank Atlas pasta machine. It has moved with us back and forth across the country a few times, and while we don't make fresh pasta as often as we would like to, when we do, it always feels like we're pulling out an old friend, and we invariably start reminiscing about past pasta making sessions…the Christmas Eve when our giant batch of homemade pasta stuck together and necessitated a last-minute trip to the store for boxed spaghetti…teaching guests to make ricotta-filled ravioli in Sicily…and the summer afternoon our friend Sydney made the most beautiful fettuccine flecked with fresh herbs—the inspiration behind this recipe, a celebration of all things allium.

FOR THE PASTA

1½ cups all-purpose flour

½ cup semolina flour

Kosher salt

2 large eggs

⅓ cup finely chopped fresh chives

Water, as needed

FOR THE SAUCE

3 tablespoons olive oil

1 bunch scallions, cut into 1-inch lengths

2 large leeks, thinly sliced

1 large sweet onion, sliced

1 large red onion, sliced

1 shallot, sliced into rounds

3 plump garlic cloves, thinly sliced

Kosher salt and freshly ground black pepper

1 cup chicken or vegetable broth

Freshly grated zest of 1 lemon

Chopped chives, for garnish

Grated Parmesan, for serving

TO MAKE THE DOUGH, STIR TOGETHER THE flours and ¼ teaspoon salt in a large bowl and make a well in the center. Gently beat the eggs and chives together in a bowl, then pour into the well. Gradually stir in the flour to form a stiff dough, adding a dribble of water if the dough is having a hard time coming together. Turn the dough out onto a lightly floured work surface and knead until firm and elastic, about 8 minutes. Wrap the dough in plastic wrap and let stand at room temperature for about 45 minutes (the dough will soften a bit as it rests).

While the dough rests, make the sauce. Combine the olive oil, scallions, leeks, sweet onion, red onion, shallots and garlic in a large skillet over moderately high heat. Season with ½ teaspoon salt and several grinds of black pepper. Cook, stirring occasionally, until softened, about 8 minutes. Add the chicken broth, reduce the heat to low, and simmer gently until onions are tender, about 10 minutes. Season to taste with salt and pepper. Cover and keep warm over very low heat while you finish the pasta.

Cut the dough in 6 equal pieces and cover with a kitchen towel. Roll out one piece of dough using a pasta roller set on the widest setting. Fold the dough in thirds, like a letter, then roll through the widest setting again. Repeat this folding and rolling on the widest setting 4 more times. Change the setting on the pasta roller to the next narrowest setting and roll the dough through once without folding. Continue changing the setting on the pasta roller, making it narrower each time, and rolling the dough through without folding until you reach the last setting. Using a sharp knife, cut the dough lengthwise into 1-inch-thick noodles. Sprinkle lightly with flour and gather into a loose nest and set aside on a floured baking sheet. Repeat with the remaining pieces of dough.

Bring a large pot of salted water to a boil. Add the pasta, stir gently to keep from sticking, and boil until tender, about 4 minutes. Using tongs, transfer the pasta to the skillet and toss well to combine. Add the lemon zest and some of the cooking water if needed to loosen the sauce. Divide the pasta and sauce among warm bowls and garnish with the chopped chives. Serve with Parmesan.

CHIVE TALKING

If you're going to attempt growing any alliums, let it be chives. They are practically foolproof and offer such satisfaction to the neophyte kitchen gardener (ahem, us). We love showering a finished dish with a handful of snipped chives—they add a beautiful hit of green and delicate onion bite—and though we admit to occasionally buying an overpriced plastic coffin of the herbs from the grocery store, most of the time we need only walk out the front door to gather a fresh handful. We have several chive plants growing in our small garden. In early spring, their green shoots are among the first to poke up, a sweet sight for winter-weary eyes. From there, chives grow quickly, produce lovely purplish flowers and can be harvested deep into the fall, until frosts set in.

Because our house is small and there's no room to cultivate plants from seed, we start chives from sets that we buy at the local farm market. We have transplanted them to pots, window boxes and directly into the ground, all with equal success. Chives prefer loose, nutrient-rich soil and are hardy enough to survive infrequent waterings. Every other spring, we dig them up and divide the clumps into smaller groupings, which we replant throughout the garden.

When snipping chives, use kitchen shears or a sharp knife to cut off a handful of outer leaves, just above the soil line. This will keep the bunch looking neat and tidy, and promote new growth. We've always regretted the times we've cut too near the tops and returned a few days later to see the chives riddled with brown stalks then curse our haste in later harvests when we end up having to pick out all those dried pieces.

CHIVE OMELET FOR ONE

We tip our hats to Elizabeth David on this one. With a little salad, a slice of toast and a glass of wine, this makes a civilized dinner for a quiet night. Crack **2 large eggs** into a bowl and beat lightly together with a fork. Whisk in **1 tablespoon finely chopped fresh chives** and a pinch of **kosher salt**. Melt **1 tablespoon butter** in a medium nonstick skillet or omelet pan over moderate heat. Pour the egg mixture into the pan, tilting the pan to cover the bottom evenly. The egg should start to set quickly. Gently lift up the edges with a rubber spatula and let some raw egg flow underneath, continuing all around until the underside is fully set but the top still looks rather runny—this will take about 30 seconds. Start rolling the omelet by scooching the spatula under one side and folding that over, continuing until the omelet is neatly rolled. Let it sit in the skillet for a few seconds more, then slide it onto a plate. Sprinkle with a few more chopped chives, if you like, and eat at once.

CHIVE SALT MAKES ABOUT 1 CUP

Use this homemade seasoning in place of plain salt over baked potatoes or popcorn. Or rub it all over a piece of meat before roasting, as in 20/20 Roast Chicken (page 184).

2 plump garlic cloves

Kosher salt

1½ cups very coarsely chopped chives

¼ cup thyme leaves

PLACE THE PEELED GARLIC CLOVES ON A cutting board and sprinkle with 1 tablespoon salt. Finely chop the garlic and salt together. Add half of the chives and thyme and continue to chop until coarsely mashed. Add the remaining chives and thyme and another 1 tablespoon salt and chop until the mixture is very finely minced. The herbs and salt may keep getting away from your knife; just gather them back in and keep chopping. By the end, there should be a grainy, green sludge smeared across your cutting board.

Transfer the mixture to a bowl and stir in 6 tablespoons salt. Spread out onto a tray and let dry overnight. If it is very humid, you may want to dry the mixture in the oven, set at the lowest temperature, for 2 to 3 hours. Transfer to a jar, seal and store at room temperature for up to 3 months.

20/20 ROAST CHICKEN
SERVES 4 TO 6

In our opinion, the classic French dish chicken with forty cloves of garlic only improves with the addition of shallots. Spatchcocking the chicken helps it to lay flat over the panful of alliums, and the two components season one another: the perfume of shallots and garlic wafts up to the bird, whose cooking juices drip back over them, creating a most intoxicating pan sauce.

1 (4-pound) chicken

3 tablespoons Chive Salt (page 183)

20 shallots

20 garlic cloves

1 tablespoon olive oil

½ cup white wine or dry vermouth

Kosher salt and freshly ground black pepper

HEAT THE OVEN TO 325°F. REMOVE THE backbone from the chicken by cutting down each side of it with kitchen shears (save the backbone to make stock if you like). Open up the chicken and tuck the wings behind the breasts. Tuck the legs in so that the bottoms of the drumsticks are pointed away from the body and the chicken is as flat as possible. Rub the chive salt all over the chicken and let sit at room temperature while you prepare the shallots and garlic.

Peel the shallots, cutting any very large ones in half. Peel the garlic cloves. Choose a baking dish in which the chicken will fit snugly. Scatter the shallots and garlic over the bottom of the dish. Arrange the chicken over top; it should almost completely cover the shallots and garlic. Rub the olive oil all over the chicken and stick in the oven. Roast for 45 minutes. Pour the wine around the chicken and return to the oven. Roast until the skin is crisp and burnished and the juices run clear, about 45 minutes more.

Transfer the chicken to a cutting board and let it rest. Skim the fat from the juices left in the dish. Using a fork, mash some of the garlic cloves to thicken the sauce; season with salt and pepper to taste.

Carve the chicken and serve with the shallots, garlic and pan sauce.

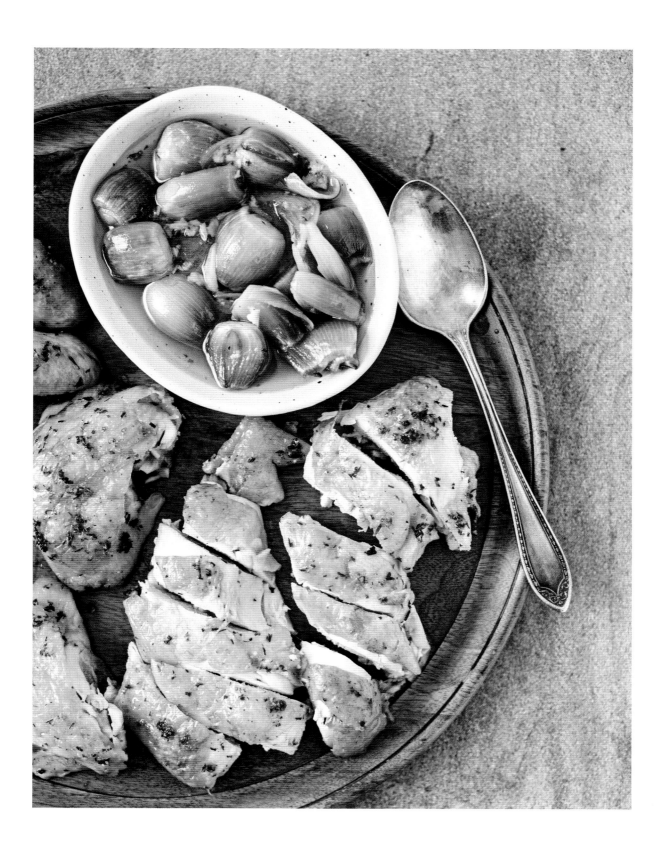

Garlic Chives. Native to eastern Asia, where they are used as much as a vegetable as an herb, garlic chives are revered for their delicate texture and forceful flavor. In the US, they are readily available in Asian markets and can be found in three different forms. The most common are bunches of the bright green leaves (which is what we use in the recipes here), which are broader, flatter and longer than those of regular chives. They may also be sold in bunches that include the buds, considered a delicacy by some.

If you grow your own garlic chives, these buds open to reveal a spray of white flowers, a gorgeous addition to a garden. Finally, you might find packages of yellow or white chives. These pale, very tender garlic chives have been blanched—that is, the grower has blocked the plant from sunlight to prevent chlorophyll from forming. No matter what type you choose, garlic chives grow very pungent over time. Store them in the refrigerator, tightly wrapped in plastic, and use within a few days.

NOODLE TOSS WITH PORK, SHREDDED TOFU AND GARLIC CHIVES SERVES 4 TO 6

This recipe started as a way to enjoy the flavors of dumplings without the finicky work of stuffing and pleating, but along the way it evolved into something a little more complicated, more complexly spiced—in a word, its own beast. But a very satisfying beast it is, like a speedy Bolognese with a Chinese bent. If you can't find garlic chives, you can substitute a bunch of scallions and 3 finely chopped garlic cloves.

8 ounces Chinese bean thread noodles or rice noodles

1 (16-ounce) block firm tofu

1 teaspoon cornstarch

1 teaspoon water

1 cup chicken broth

¼ cup soy sauce

1 tablespoon mirin

1 teaspoon sambal oelek or other chile garlic sauce

1 teaspoon toasted sesame oil

1 cup chopped garlic chives

1 to 2 fresh hot chiles, thinly sliced

1-inch piece fresh ginger, finely chopped

1 teaspoon ground Sichuan peppercorns, optional

2 tablespoons peanut or vegetable oil

1 pound ground pork

Kosher salt

PUT THE NOODLES IN A LARGE BOWL OF cold water and set aside to soak while you prepare the rest of the ingredients.

Using a box grater, coarsely shred the tofu into a colander or sieve and set over a bowl to drain. Place a small plate on top of the tofu and weigh down with a can or jar. Set aside with the noodles.

Combine the cornstarch and 1 teaspoon water in a 2-cup measuring cup and stir to dissolve. Add the chicken broth, soy sauce, mirin, sambal oelek and sesame oil to the slurry and whisk together.

Combine the garlic chives, chiles, ginger and Sichuan peppercorns, if using, in a bowl. Drain the noodles.

Heat the peanut oil in a large wok or heavy skillet over high heat. Add the chopped chive mixture to the hot wok and fry, stirring, until very fragrant, about 30 seconds. Add the pork, breaking up the meat into small clumps with the spatula, season lightly with salt and fry until no longer pink, 5 to 6 minutes. Add the shredded tofu, toss to combine, and cook for a couple of minutes more. Whisk the broth mixture to ensure the cornstarch is well combined and pour into the wok. Bring to a boil, then add the noodles and cook, stirring from time to time, until the noodles are tender, about 5 minutes. Serve at once, with extra sambal oelek on the side.

PORK AND GARLIC CHIVE POTSTICKERS MAKES ABOUT 2 DOZEN DUMPLINGS

When we lived in New York, we usually kept a stash of pork and chive dumplings in the freezer. A bag of fifty dumplings cost about $8, and we loved slipping into the little dumpling shops off Mott Street to watch the women at work. Using chopsticks, they'd snag the perfect amount of filling from a giant stainless steel bowl then tuck it into the wrapper in their palm and deftly seal the dumpling with a half-dozen perfect pleats, all in about twenty seconds. Having dumplings in the freezer was like money in the bank—until our consciences crept up on us. We finally acknowledged that dumplings that cheap couldn't be good for us, nor for the animal providing the meat. So we started making our own with good-quality pork. We'll never be as nimble and quick as the Mott Street maestras, but we get better with each batch. You will, too.

1 pound ground pork

½ cup chopped garlic chives

½-inch piece fresh ginger, minced

2 tablespoons soy sauce

1 teaspoon toasted sesame oil

All-purpose flour for dusting

24 to 30 round dumpling wrappers, defrosted if frozen

2 tablespoons peanut or vegetable oil

COMBINE THE PORK, GARLIC CHIVES, ginger, soy sauce and sesame oil in a bowl and knead the mixture until well combined.

Line a large baking sheet with paper towels and dust lightly with flour. Take 1 dumpling wrapper and place about 2 teaspoons pork mixture in the center. Fold the dough over the filling to form an open half moon shape. With a wet finger, moisten the lower inner edge of the wrapper. To seal, using the thumb and forefinger of one hand, form 6 to 8 tiny pleats along the unmoistened edge of the wrapper, pressing the pleats against the moistened border to enclose filling. The moistened border will stay smooth and will automatically curve in the distinctive semicircular shape of dumplings. Stand the dumpling, seam-side up, on the baking sheet and gently press to flatten the bottom. Cover loosely with a dampened cloth or paper towel. Form the remaining dumplings in the same manner.

Heat the oil in a medium nonstick skillet over moderately high heat until hot but not smoking. Quickly arrange the potstickers in a tight circular pattern—it's okay if they touch one another—and cook, uncovered, until the bottoms are pale golden, 2 to 3 minutes. Add ½ cup water to the skillet, cover tightly and reduce the heat to moderate. Cook until the liquid has evaporated and the bottoms of the dumplings are crisp and golden, 7 to 10 minutes. Add a little more water if the skillet looks dry before the bottoms are browned. Remove the lid and cook, shaking the skillet to loosen the potstickers, until the steam dissipates, 1 to 2 minutes. Invert a large plate over the skillet. Using pot holders, hold the plate and skillet together and invert, so that the crisp browned bottoms of the potstickers are face up. Serve right away.

DEARLY BELOVEDS

SHALLOTS & LEEKS

Shallots. They are thought to have originated near Palestine, but it's fun to imagine these small alliums migrating across a world map to the two places we now most associate with them: France and Southeast Asia. In French cooking, shallots are revered for their role in vinaigrettes and sauces, while in Thailand, Laos and Vietnam, shallots go to work flavoring chile pastes, broths and curries. Crisp paper-thin rounds of deep-fried shallots are sprinkled over many Southeast Asian dishes, a tradition that makes anything and everything taste terrific.

Depending on the cultivar, shallots can be long and tapering or plump and round, with skin colors that range from copper to gold to gray. Their white crisp flesh is tinged with pink or violet and is quite mild in flavor compared to regular storage onions. Shallots often grow in clusters of two bulbs lightly attached at the root. When separated, that flat side makes for easy chopping. One of the many things we love about shallots is their compact size—if a recipe calls for only a little bit of onion, one medium shallot will often provide the perfect amount.

Shallots are quite expensive, compared to other onions, so choose carefully and look for ones that are firm and heavy with tight skins and no sprouting greens. Store them in a dry, well-ventilated spot. We always keep a few shallots on hand for our weekly vinaigrette but stock up when we are making something that calls for lots, like Vadouvan (page 117) or Black Pepper Chicken Skewers (page 214).

PERFECT SHALLOT VINAIGRETTE

MAKES ABOUT ½ CUP, ENOUGH
FOR 4 SERVINGS OF GREEN SALAD

We make green salads several times a week, and you'll often find an old jam jar filled with this classic dressing sitting out on our kitchen counter. If company's coming, we'll whisk together a fresh batch in the bottom of a salad bowl, then top with the greens and toss just before we're ready to eat. If faced with the dregs of a jar of mustard, just make the dressing in the jar. If you can't tell, we're a little obsessed with it. It's worth taking the time to let the shallots sit for a bit in the mustard and vinegar. It will greatly temper their bite.

1 medium shallot, finely chopped

1 teaspoon Dijon mustard

1 tablespoon sherry, white or red wine vinegar

Kosher salt and freshly ground black pepper

¼ cup olive oil

WHISK TOGETHER THE SHALLOTS, MUSTARD, vinegar, ¼ teaspoon salt and several grinds of black pepper. Whisk in the olive oil. Taste and adjust the seasonings as you like. Alternately, combine everything in a glass jar, seal and shake, shake, shake until well combined.

NOTES: On the rare occasion that we don't have a shallot in the house, we happily use a quarter of a red onion, finely chopped, in its place. Finely chopped scallion also works nicely. For something a bit bolder, we use a Microplane to finely grate a garlic clove in place of the shallot. To go mellower, simply mash up a garlic clove and let it sit in the dressing to fragrance it.

MIGNONETTE SAUCE

MAKES ABOUT ½ CUP, ENOUGH FOR 1 TO 2 DOZEN OYSTERS

Guy's father, uncle and grandfather all had their own fish markets in New Jersey, and as a teenager, Guy and his dad often made the early-morning trip to the Fulton Fish Market (then in lower Manhattan) to pick up the day's order. He believes that really fresh, lively oysters need little embellishment, but sometimes a dab of sharpness is just the thing to balance the salinity of the shellfish.

This classic sauce comes from American seafood expert and chef Barton Seaver. We love his idea of combining black pepper and allspice—to do so, crush equal parts black peppercorns and allspice berries in a pepper grinder or with a small mortar and pestle.

1 medium shallot, very finely chopped

3 tablespoons red wine vinegar

Kosher salt

1 tablespoon water

⅛ teaspoon freshly ground black pepper and allspice

COMBINE THE SHALLOTS, VINEGAR AND PINCH of salt in a small bowl and let sit while you shuck the oysters, 10 to 15 minutes.

Just before serving, stir in the water and the pepper-allspice blend. Drizzle a small spoonful (an espresso spoon is handy) of the mignonette sauce over an oyster and slurp immediately.

STEPHANIE'S PICKLED SHALLOTS MAKES 2 CUPS

During a late-night scroll through Facebook, a friend's photo of these pickles caught our eye. We texted her, she texted the recipe back and two days later, we were eating them—and honestly, we haven't stopped since. They make any sandwich, especially an egg salad shmear or BLT, taste unforgettable. Make sure to scoop up some of the pickled coriander and juniper berries when you grab the shallots—they impart a pleasant crunch and perfumed pop to the proceedings.

5 to 7 large shallots

2 tablespoons coriander seeds

1 tablespoon juniper berries

2 whole cloves

¾ cup apple cider vinegar

¼ cup firmly packed light brown sugar

¼ cup water

Kosher salt

THINLY SLICE THE SHALLOTS, PACKING THEM into a clean pint jar as you work, stopping when the jar is full. Combine the coriander, juniper and cloves in a small skillet and toast over moderate heat, stirring all the while, until fragrant, 1 to 2 minutes. Remove from the heat and add to the shallots.

Add the vinegar, brown sugar, water and 1 teaspoon salt to the skillet and bring to a boil over moderately high heat, stirring until the sugar and salt are dissolved. Carefully pour the boiling brine over the shallots and spices. Let cool to room temperature, then seal and refrigerate at least overnight before serving. The shallots will keep for several months in the fridge.

FRIED SHALLOTS WITH A BONUS OF SHALLOT OIL

MAKES ABOUT 3 CUPS FRIED SHALLOTS AND 1 CUP SHALLOT OIL

Crisply fried slivers of shallot are a traditional topping for all sorts of Southeast Asian dishes, and you can buy them by the tub at Asian supermarkets. Or you can make your own. Good luck not snacking through the whole batch before they make it to their final resting place. We scatter them over salads, noodles, curries and grilled meats. Use the oil in stir-fries, salad dressings and for drizzling over Congee (page 175).

1 pound shallots

1½ cups peanut or vegetable oil

PEEL THE SHALLOTS AND SLICE THEM VERY thinly. Transfer to a bowl and use your fingers to gently separate the rings as much as possible. Line a large platter with paper towels.

Heat the oil in a small heavy pot to 350°F. Working in batches, add a handful of shallots to the oil and fry, stirring all the while with a slotted spoon, until the shallots are well browned, 2 to 2½ minutes. Using the slotted spoon, transfer the shallots to the lined platter to drain. Repeat with the remaining shallots. Make sure the oil comes back up to 350°F between batches. The shallots will crisp up as they cool. Once cooled, they can be transferred to an airtight container and kept at room temperature for up to 1 week.

Let the oil cool, then pour through a fine-mesh sieve into a glass jar. Seal and store for up to 1 month in the refrigerator.

BURMESE SEED SALAD WITH BASIL DRESSING SERVES 6 TO 8

Mu Jing Lau, owner of the fantastic Pan-Asian restaurant Mu Du Noodles in Santa Fe, shared a version of this recipe years ago. It is one of the most interesting, satisfying salads we've ever made. Each bite bounces between crunch and juice, from sweet to nutty—it's the perfect thing for a hot summer day, or a tropical pick-me-up on a cold winter one.

FOR THE DRESSING

1 cup basil leaves

2 garlic cloves, coarsely chopped

1-inch piece fresh ginger, coarsely chopped

¼ cup freshly squeezed orange juice

¼ cup Brazil nuts or walnuts

2 tablespoons rice vinegar

1 teaspoon toasted sesame oil

½ cup grapeseed oil

1 medium shallot, finely chopped

Kosher salt

FOR THE SALAD

1 small head napa or green cabbage

Kosher salt

2 ruby red grapefruits

½ cup pickled ginger, drained and thinly sliced

½ cup roasted pumpkin seeds

½ cup roasted sunflower seeds

½ cup roasted soy nuts

½ cup roasted peanuts

¼ cup lightly toasted sesame seeds

1 cup Fried Shallots (page 205)

TO MAKE THE DRESSING, BRING A SMALL POT of water to a boil. Place the basil leaves in a sieve and dunk in the boiling water until bright green, about 15 seconds. Run under cold water to cool and set the color, then squeeze the leaves as dry as possible. Transfer the basil to a blender, along with the garlic, ginger, orange juice, Brazil nuts, rice vinegar and sesame oil. Blend on high until very smooth. While the blender is running, add the grapeseed oil in a slow stream and blend until smooth. Transfer the dressing to a measuring cup and stir in the chopped shallots. Season the dressing with salt, starting with ½ teaspoon and adding more to taste if needed. Set aside.

To make the salad, very thinly slice enough cabbage leaves to measure about 8 cups. Toss the cabbage with 1 teaspoon salt in a large bowl and let sit while you prepare the rest of the salad.

Peel the grapefruits and chop the flesh: cut off all the peel and pith with a sharp knife. Working over a bowl to collect the juice, cut the segments free from the membranes. Chop the segments and add to the bowl of juice.

Drain off any liquid that has collected in the bottom of the bowl of cabbage. Pour the dressing over the cabbage and toss well to coat. Add the pickled ginger and the grapefruit, including its juice, to the cabbage and toss gently; don't worry if the grapefruit breaks up into small strands. Scatter the pumpkin seeds, sunflower seeds, soy nuts, peanuts, and sesame seeds over the salad and toss once more. Taste the salad and add a little salt if needed. Divide among plates and top each serving with a handful of fried shallots.

SYLVIE'S THAI CUCUMBER SALAD SERVES 6

When we lived in Santa Fe, we were part of a close-knit group of friends who loved to gather for meals, especially on warm summer evenings when dusk seemed to linger forever. Our good friend Sylvie brought this salad to one of those dinners, and every time we've made it since, we think back on those expansive days of friendship—a testament to how food and memory are so intimately connected. This salad touches upon all the major tastes—sweet, salty, tart and spicy—and you'll find you can't stop eating it. It's just the thing with chicken satay, grilled pork chops or as part of a rice bowl.

½ cup sugar

½ cup white vinegar

½ cup water

Kosher salt

3 cucumbers

2 large shallots, finely chopped

1 jalapeño, finely chopped

¼ cup salted peanuts, chopped

Handful of fresh mint, finely chopped

Handful of fresh cilantro, finely chopped

COMBINE THE SUGAR, VINEGAR, WATER AND 1 teaspoon salt in a small saucepan over moderately high heat and bring to a gentle boil, stirring until the sugar and salt are dissolved. Remove from the heat and cool to room temperature.

Peel the cucumbers and halve them lengthwise. If the cucumbers are very seedy, scrape out the seeds with the tip of a spoon. Slice the cucumbers crosswise and put in a large bowl. Add the shallots and jalapeño to the cucumbers. Pour the dressing over the vegetables and stir well to combine. Refrigerate until very cold, about 3 hours.

Just before serving, sprinkle the peanuts, mint and cilantro over the salad.

GRILLED DELICATA SQUASH WITH SHALLOT AGRODOLCE SERVES 6

During the winter, we eat a lot of hardy squashes. Like most cooks, we usually cut them into wedges or cubes, throw them in oven until they're caramelized and tender and call it done. During our stay in Sicily, Fabrizia Lanza made us a dish of grilled winter squash that forced us to look at the vegetable in a completely different way and showed off the depth and subtlety of Sicilian food. Cooking sliced delicata rings quickly over a grill produces squash that still has a bit of snap and a flavorful hint of its vegetal roots, one that doesn't surrender completely to its sugary nature.

2 delicata squash

Kosher salt

3 shallots, sliced

¼ cup olive oil

¼ cup golden raisins

¼ cup white wine vinegar

1 tablespoon sugar

Freshly ground black pepper

CUT OFF ONE END OF EACH OF THE squashes to reveal the seeds and core. Using a long-handled spoon, scrape out the seeds and discard (or save for another use). Cut the squash crosswise into ¼-inch-thick slices.

Heat a grill or a grill pan over moderate heat. Do not oil the grates of the grill or the pan, but make sure they are very clean. Have a platter and a piece of foil on hand. Dry-grill the squash until charred on one side, about 5 minutes, then use tongs to flip the squash and continue to cook until the slices are well browned and almost tender, about 5 minutes more. As the slices are grilled, transfer them to a platter and cover with foil. Season lightly with salt and keep tightly covered while you make the agrodolce.

Combine the shallots and olive oil in a skillet over moderate heat and cook, stirring from time to time, until softened and golden brown in spots, about 10 minutes. Stir in the raisins, vinegar, sugar, 1 teaspoon salt and several grinds of black pepper and simmer until the mixture has reduced to a juicy glaze, about 2 minutes. Immediately pour the shallot mixture over the squash and let sit at room temperature for at least 1 hour before serving.

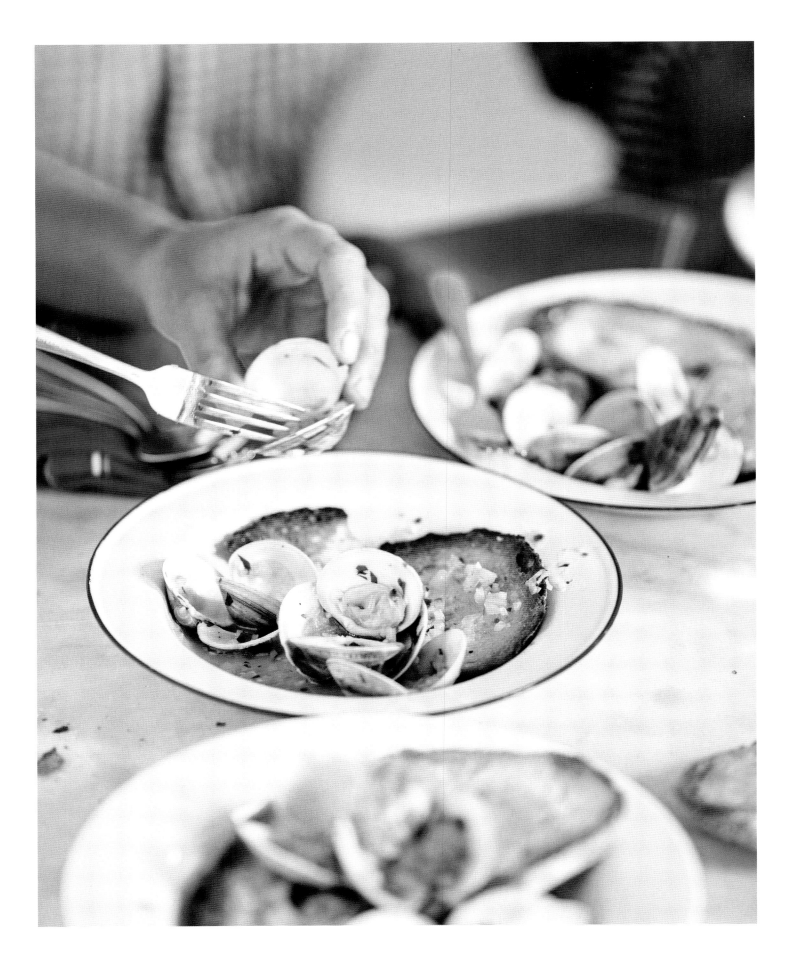

STEAMED CLAMS WITH SHALLOTS AND GARLIC SERVES 4 TO 6

For a few years, we spent a week every summer visiting friends in Marion, Massachusetts, a small all-American town overlooking Buzzards Bay. Their house had a fabulous kitchen with an industrial six-burner stove, which is where you could find us when we weren't at the beach, taking a walk or reading/napping on the couch. During one of those spirited kitchen nights, we made a huge pot of steamed clams, and Andrew, a Massachusetts native and resident expert on local seafood, added a last-minute pinch of freshly grated lemon zest to the broth. That little trick made the whole dish sparkle—we had no idea what we'd been missing!

4 dozen small clams

8 tablespoons unsalted butter or ½ cup olive oil

3 large shallots, finely chopped

6 plump garlic cloves, finely chopped

¼ teaspoon crushed red pepper flakes

Freshly ground black pepper

1 cup dry white wine

1 tablespoon finely chopped flat-leaf parsley

Freshly grated zest of 1 lemon

Garlicky Garlic Bread (page 291) or cooked linguine, for serving

SCRUB THE CLAMS WELL AND SET ASIDE IN a colander.

Melt the butter in a heavy pot over moderately high heat. When the butter foams, add the shallots and garlic and cook, stirring from time to time, until softened, about 5 minutes. (Or combine the olive oil, shallots and garlic in the pot and heat together over moderately high heat.) Stir in the red pepper flakes and several grinds of black pepper, then pour in the wine and bring to a boil. As soon as the mixture boils, add the clams and cover the pot. Cook the clams, stirring once, until they open wide, about 5 minutes. Discard any clams that don't open, then stir in the parsley and lemon zest. Remove from the heat and serve the clams in warmed shallow bowls with the garlic toast or over linguine.

BLACK PEPPER CHICKEN SKEWERS SERVES 6

Yotam Ottolenghi's recipe for tofu cooked with tons of black pepper and alliums has become a well-deserved classic—its flavors are so bold and brash. We streamlined the recipe and substituted meaty chicken thighs for the tofu, but this dish will still wake you right up. Skewering the chicken helps it brown evenly and makes it easy to take in and out of the skillet. (Incidentally, the skewered meat also reminds us of a real Pittsburgh mainstay called city chicken—actually pork!—that could not be more different in flavor or temperament.) Steamed white rice and Sylvie's Thai Cucumber Salad (page 209) are a nice way to round out the meal. Get everything prepped before you approach the stove. Once you start cooking, it all comes together very quickly.

3 tablespoons black peppercorns

3 pounds skinless, boneless chicken thighs

Kosher salt

½ cup soy sauce

1 tablespoon honey

6 tablespoons butter

15 small shallots, thinly sliced

9 plump garlic cloves, finely chopped

3-inch piece fresh ginger, finely chopped

1 to 2 fresh chiles, such as bird's eye, cayenne, serrano or jalapeño, thinly sliced

4 scallions, thinly sliced

Steamed white rice, for serving

1 lime, halved plus lime wedges for serving

USING A SPICE GRINDER OR MORTAR AND pestle, coarsely grind the peppercorns. Cut the chicken into 1-inch chunks and thread evenly on bamboo skewers (6-inch skewers fit easily into a skillet). Season the chicken all over with salt and some of the pepper you just ground. Combine the soy sauce and honey and stir together until the honey has dissolved.

Heat the butter in a large heavy skillet over moderately high heat. When it foams, add the chicken skewers in batches and cook, turning occasionally, until browned all over, 8 to 10 minutes. Transfer the skewers to a plate.

Add the shallots, garlic, ginger and chiles to the skillet, reduce the heat to moderate and cook, stirring from time to time and scraping up any leftover chicken bits from the bottom of the pan, until the vegetables are softened, about 5 minutes. Stir in the soy sauce and honey, as well as the remaining ground black pepper, and cook for about 1 minute.

Return the chicken skewers to the skillet, along with any juices that have collected on the plate. Cook the chicken until it is cooked through and well coated with the sticky sauce, about 3 minutes more. Remove from the heat. Squeeze the lime over the dish and scatter with the sliced scallions. Serve with white rice and lime wedges.

Leeks. The emperor Nero was such a fan that he earned the nickname *Porrophagus*, or "leek eater" (*porrum* is Latin for leek). To this day, the leek is a symbol of Wales, whose soldiers tied leeks to their helmets to distinguish themselves from the invading Saxons. They certainly deserved to win—imagine going into battle with a twelve-inch leek strapped to your head!

In ancient times, leeks were highly prized for their mildness and sweetness and considered more of a vegetable than just a seasoning, as onions and garlic were. Today, leeks persist in having a more elevated social status than their humble cousin the storage onion and are among the more expensive alliums in the market. Maybe it's their long, slender good looks. Although they look like giant scallions, with an elongated white bulb sheathed in broad, flat green leaves, leeks generally are not good raw, needing a little heat and attention to come to life. They take very well to cream and butter, as in creamed leeks or vichyssoise, arguably the best-known leek dish, but a little sharpness in the form of vinaigrette or something like a romesco sauce can be even more interesting.

Leeks are in season from fall through spring, but are readily available year round. When shopping, choose bunches with similarly sized leeks, especially if you plan to poach and serve them whole—that way they will cook at the same rate. Also, look for leeks with the longest white stems, but don't be afraid to inch into the greens. To achieve these long, white stalks, farmers deprive the plant of sunlight by trenching it—mounding soil up around the leek as it grows—or by tying paper around the stem. We often discard the outer leaves from the middle of the leek and see if we can salvage a bit more of the tender inner stalk. In any case, you can save the greens and add them to stocks. To store them, wrap the leeks loosely in plastic and stash them in the crisper, where they will last up to a week. Cut some extra length from the greens first so they fit more easily in your fridge.

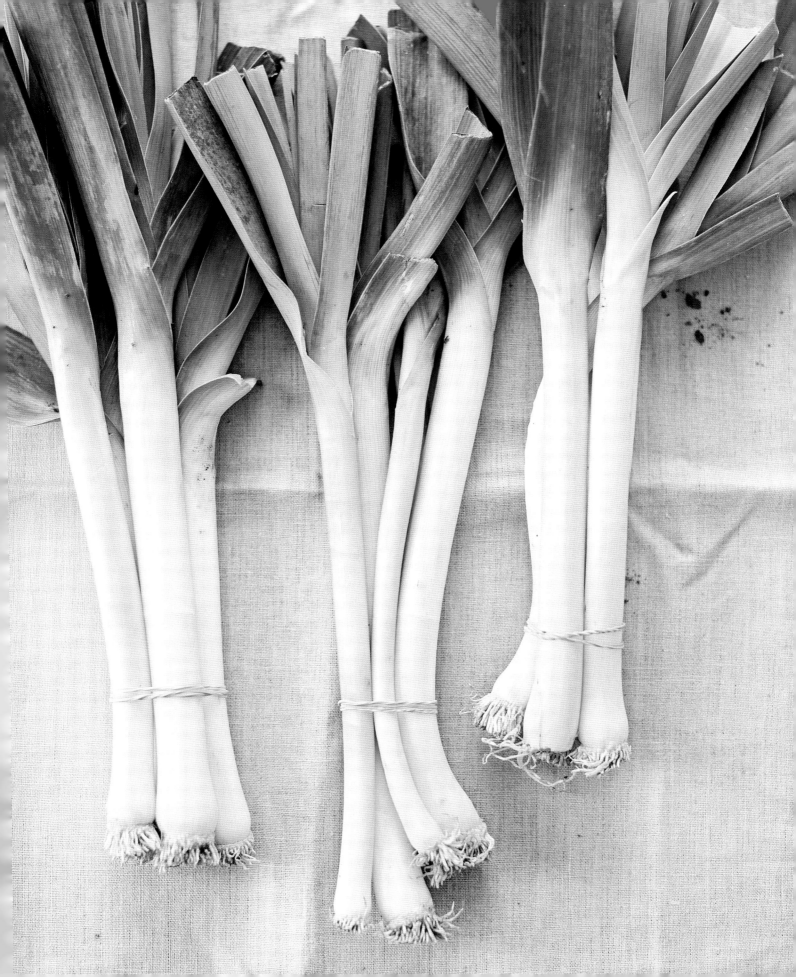

LEEK TART WITH FETA AND DILL SERVES 6

Kate spent her college years happily working at a little Greek restaurant in Charlottesville, Virginia, and the scents of dill and feta have a Proustian effect on her. There's an easy elegance about this low-slung tart that combines those two flavors with leeks in an unfussy custard of eggs and yogurt. When preparing the dough, consider doubling the recipe and stashing half of it in the freezer. You'll be happy knowing it's there, ready at a moment's notice so you can make another treat like Pearl Onion Tarte Tatin (page 235) or Red Onion Goat Cheese Galette (page 84).

FOR THE DOUGH

1½ cups all-purpose flour

Kosher salt

8 tablespoons cold butter, cut into pieces

3 to 4 tablespoons ice water

FOR THE FILLING

2 large leeks, thinly sliced

1 tablespoon olive oil

Kosher salt and freshly ground black pepper

3 large eggs

¾ cup Greek yogurt

½ cup crumbled feta

1 tablespoon finely chopped fresh dill

Freshly grated nutmeg

TO MAKE THE DOUGH, COMBINE THE FLOUR and ¼ teaspoon salt in a bowl and, using your hands or a pastry cutter, quickly work in the butter until the floury mixture is filled with pea-sized lumps. Drizzle 3 tablespoons ice water over the mixture and stir with your hands or a fork to combine until the dough just holds together when squeezed. Add the remaining water if necessary. Gather the dough into a ball and flatten slightly, then wrap tightly in plastic wrap. Refrigerate for at least 1 hour and up to a couple of days.

When you're ready to bake the tart, heat the oven to 375°F. Roll the dough out on a lightly floured countertop into a generous round, about 11 inches in diameter. Fit it into an 8- or 9-inch round tart pan with a removable bottom by loosely rolling the dough around the rolling pin and then unfurling it over the pan. Trim the edge, leaving a 1-inch overhang, then tuck the overhanging dough into the pan, pressing it against the sides to reinforce them. Prick the base of the tart all over with a fork. Line with a large sheet of parchment and fill with pie weights (we use a combination of dried beans and rice). Bake for 15 minutes, then carefully remove the parchment and beans. Bake the empty pastry shell for 10 minutes more; the crust should be golden and set.

While the pastry is baking, make the filling. Combine the leeks and olive oil in a large skillet, season with ½ teaspoon salt and several grinds of black pepper, and cook over moderately high heat, stirring often, until just softened, about 5 minutes. Remove from the heat.

Crack the eggs into a bowl and gently whisk until well combined. Whisk in the yogurt, feta, dill and a grating of nutmeg. Scrape the leeks into the bowl and stir together. Set the tart pan on a foil-lined baking sheet in case the filling leaks. Pour the egg mixture into the tart shell and bake until set and the edges are golden brown, 30 to 35 minutes. Remove from the oven and serve warm or at room temperature.

LEEKS VINAIGRETTE WITH EGG MIMOSA SERVES 4

Kate ate leeks vinaigrette for the first time as a teenager in France. Compared to the onion rings she grew up on, those leeks were a revelation—like hearing Piaf for the first time after a steady diet of Bon Jovi. We like to make this with slender, tender leeks from a local farm. They're just right for this delicate presentation.

Trim **1 bunch (4 to 6) slender leeks** so that they fit in a large skillet. Halve the leeks lengthwise almost to the root. Rinse well under cold running water, fanning out the layers to release any dirt or grit. Arrange the leeks in the skillet; don't worry if you need to bend them a bit to fit. Cover with cold water, season well with **kosher salt** and drop in **4 or 5 black peppercorns**. Cover the skillet and bring to a simmer. Simmer until the leeks yield easily when pierced with the tip of a sharp knife, 5 to 6 minutes from the time the water comes to a simmer, though this will depend upon the thickness of your leeks. Remove from the heat and rinse the leeks well under cold running water to stop the cooking and preserve their color. (Or, if you managed to think ahead, dunk the leeks in a bowl of ice water.) Drain well, pat the leeks dry and arrange on a platter. Make **1 batch Perfect Shallot Vinaigrette (page 199)**. If you like, finely chop **1 or 2 anchovy fillets** and stir into the vinaigrette. Spoon the vinaigrette over the leeks. Finely chop **1 hard-boiled egg** (or push it through a sieve) and scatter the crumbles over the leeks, along with some **finely chopped flat-leaf parsley**.

IT'S A DIRTY JOB, BUT SOMEONE HAS TO DO IT

A surprising amount of silt can hide in a leek's layers, and one bite of missed grit can throw you off a whole dish. Depending on the recipe, we wash leeks one of two ways. If they're meant to be served whole or halved, as in Leeks Vinaigrette with Egg Mimosa (above), trim them, discarding the tough green tops. Cut the leeks in half lengthwise, almost to the root end, and then rinse under cold running water, fanning out the layers between your fingers and letting the water sluice through each layer. If they are to be chopped or julienned, cut as directed in the recipe. Fill a large bowl with cold water and add the chopped leeks, swishing them around and separating the layers with your fingers. Once the specks of dirt have settled to the bottom of the bowl, carefully lift out the leeks, taking care not to include any of the dirt. If the leeks are especially grubby, you may need to wash them a second time.

FRIZZLED LEEKS MAKES ABOUT 1 CUP

Use these crisp matchsticks as an elegant topper for grilled steak, soups or mashed potatoes. Thinly slice the white and light green parts of **1 medium leek** into julienne strips, about 3 inches long. Rinse well to remove any grit, drain and pat dry. Heat about 1 inch **peanut oil** in a small saucepan over moderately high heat to 350°F on a deep-fry thermometer. Add a small handful of leeks to the oil and fry, stirring often with a slotted spoon, until light golden brown, 60 to 90 seconds. Lift out the leeks, letting excess oil drain back into the saucepan, and transfer to a paper towel-lined plate. Repeat with the remaining leeks. Sprinkle the leeks lightly with kosher salt while still hot. Cool to room temperature before using as a garnish.

CHEESE AND ALLIUM TOASTIES
MAKES 18 TO 22 SMALL SANDWICHES

These little golden sandwiches are based on the allium-filled grilled cheese on the menu at Kappacasein Dairy, a London cheesemaker. The bite of finely chopped leeks, onion and garlic is a welcome foil to the rich cheese. They make a great appetizer, or serve a stack with cups of tomato soup. We sometimes lose the lid (and the butter) and make these open-face, just running them under the broiler until the cheese is melted and bubbly.

Shred **6 ounces good-quality sharp Cheddar cheese**. In a separate bowl, stir together **⅓ cup finely chopped leek** (white part only), **⅓ cup finely chopped red onion** and **2 finely chopped garlic cloves**. Cut **1 sourdough baguette** on the diagonal into very thin (about ¼-inch-thick) slices. Lavishly spread one side of each baguette slice with **softened salted butter**. Arrange as many slices of baguette, buttered sides down, as will fit on a sandwich press or in a heavy skillet. Top each slice with 1 heaping tablespoon of the cheese mixture and 1 heaping teaspoon of the onion mixture, then top with a second slice of bread, buttered side up.

Turn on the sandwich press and cook over moderate heat until the bread is crisp and golden brown and the cheese is melted, about 4 minutes. Repeat with the remaining ingredients to make more toasties. If toasting the sandwiches in a skillet, cook over moderate heat until the undersides are golden brown, then flip and continue to cook until golden brown and gooey.

WHITE LEEK SOUP SERVES 6

This soup creates a pale, velvety canvas for a host of embellishments: try a scattering of Frizzled Leeks (page 222), Stephanie's Pickled Shallots (page 202), a dollop of yogurt and snipped chives, Pickled Ramps (page 260) or a few pieces of Dilly Garlic Scapes (page 275). Spice things up with chopped Easiest Kimchi (page 163) or a simple squirt of sriracha and a drizzle of toasted sesame oil. If you make this ahead and reheat it, you'll want to thin it out with a bit of water; the celery root makes this soup extremely silky, but also tends to thicken it as it sits.

2 fat leeks, chopped

2 tablespoons olive oil

2 white sweet potatoes, peeled and chopped

1 medium celery root, peeled and chopped

1 fat parsnip, peeled and chopped

1 russet potato, peeled and chopped

Kosher salt

8 cups water

COMBINE THE LEEKS AND OLIVE OIL IN HEAVY pot over moderate heat and cook gently until softened, stirring from time to time, about 5 minutes. Add the sweet potatoes, celery root, parsnip and russet potato, stirring to coat with the oil. Season with 2 teaspoons salt and add the water. Bring to a boil then lower the heat and simmer gently until the vegetables are very tender, 30 to 40 minutes.

Remove the soup from the heat and purée it until very smooth, using either a hand blender or working in batches with a regular blender (use caution when blending hot liquids; the steam may build up pressure that can pop the top of the blender off). Taste the soup and add a bit more salt if needed. Serve warm.

LAMB STEW WITH FAVAS, TURNIPS AND LEEKS SERVES 6

It's natural to think about making this dish in the spring with fresh favas and the first sweet turnips of the year. But as with most stews, we're more drawn to it in the fall. That's when turnips and leeks return to the market, but we've also started wandering down the frozen foods aisle of our supermarket. Goya frozen fava beans are a wonderful, affordable treat. If you can't find favas fresh or frozen, cooked chickpeas or white beans make a fine substitute. We season the stew with the Tunisian spice paste Hrous (page 56), but Harissa (page 300) also works. That makes it a little more fiery, which might be just the thing.

2 to 2½ pounds leg of lamb

Kosher salt and freshly ground black pepper

3 tablespoons olive oil

1 big bunch leeks, halved lengthwise and thinly sliced

6 plump cloves garlic, chopped

¼ cup Hrous (page 56)

1 teaspoon ground cumin

2 cups water

1 pound shelled fresh or frozen fava beans

1 bunch small Hakurei turnips with their greens

CUT THE LAMB INTO 1½-INCH PIECES, CUT-ting around the bone if necessary. (If there is a bone, keep it and add it to the stew for extra flavor.) Generously season the meat all over with salt and pepper.

Heat the olive oil in a large Dutch oven or heavy pot over high heat and, working in batches, brown the meat all over, about 3 minutes per batch. Transfer the browned meat to a dish.

Reduce the heat to moderate and add the leeks. Cook, scraping the bottom of the pot, until the leeks are softened, about 5 minutes. Stir in the garlic, hrous and cumin and cook for 1 minute. Return the lamb and any juices collected in the dish to the pot and give a good stir so that the meat is fully coated with the spice and leek mixture. Add the water, bring to a simmer then cover tightly and reduce the heat to moderately low. Cook until the lamb is very tender, about 2 hours.

While the lamb cooks, bring a pot of water to a boil and drop in the shelled fava beans. Blanch for 1 minute then drain well and rinse under cold running water. Pinch off the skins and discard. Set the peeled fava beans aside.

Separate the greens from the turnips and wash both well. Chop the greens and set aside. Trim the turnips and halve them, or quarter them if large. When the lamb is tender, drop in the turnips, adding a bit more water if needed. Cook until the turnips are tender, about 15 minutes, then stir in the fava beans and turnip greens and cook about 10 minutes more. Taste and adjust the seasonings as needed.

CHRISTINE'S VERDURETTE MAKES ABOUT 6 CUPS

As with so many good food things, we learned of this versatile, salt-preserved blend from Guy's sister Christine. Think of it as a sort of fresh bouillon cube that adds instant flavor and keeps for months in the fridge. Rub the mixture on chicken or a piece of fish before roasting. Toss cubes of winter squash with it before sliding them into the oven. Add a scoop of verdurette to cannellini beans as they simmer away. We have spread it under the skin of a Thanksgiving turkey and made delicious gravy from the drippings. The general idea is that you use equal proportions of leeks, celery, celery root and salt, plus another measure of herbs, garlic and dried mushrooms.

½ ounce dried mushrooms, such as maitake or porcini

1 bunch celery

1 small or ½ large celery root

3 medium leeks, well washed

1 small red onion

1 head garlic

1 big bunch flat-leaf parsley

Large handful fresh sage leaves

1 cup kosher salt

PLACE THE DRIED MUSHROOMS IN A SMALL bowl and pour a cupful of hot water over them. Place a saucer over the mushrooms to keep them submerged and set aside to soak while you prepare the rest of the ingredients.

Chop the celery into large chunks, then pulse in a food processor until finely chopped. Scrape the chopped celery into a large bowl (don't worry about cleaning out the processor bowl). Peel the celery root and chop it into large chunks; pulse in the processor until finely chopped. Scrape into the bowl with the celery. Continue trimming, peeling, chopping and processing the leeks, onion, garlic, parsley and sage—one at a time—and transferring them to the large bowl.

Drain the mushrooms (reserve the soaking liquid for another use if you like, such as risotto or soup) and rinse well to release any trapped grit. Squeeze dry, then pulse in the food processor until finely chopped and add to the bowl. Stir all the vegetables and herbs together, then stir in the salt until evenly combined. Pack the verdurette into clean glass jars, seal and store in the refrigerator, where it will keep for several months.

PEARL ONIONS & CIPOLLINI

Pearl Onions. Dainty specimens whose bulbs are only about an inch in diameter, pearl onions have a mild, sweet flavor and crisp, juicy flesh. They are usually sold in small mesh bags and are available year round. Close to the holidays, stores may carry a trio of pearl onion varieties—white, yellow and red—but the rest of the year often only white is available. They are planted very tightly together so their growth is stunted, resulting in the diminutive size. Top-setting onions, also known as Egyptian or walking onions, can be used as pearl onions, but this variety grows quite differently, forming clustered bulbils at the top of the flower stalk rather than a single onion under the ground. Sometimes referred to as cocktail onions, pearls are often pickled and used to garnish drinks, most notably the gin martini known as the Gibson. Their bite-sized nature also makes them perfect for adding to stews and for grilling.

Peeling these little guys always takes longer than you think it will. Prepare yourself as you should for any thankless kitchen task: either approach this as a meditation or put on a good podcast. When we're very short on time, we grab frozen bags of already-peeled onions and consider it money well spent.

PEARL ONION TARTE TATIN SERVES 6

Before you start, place your raw onions in the skillet and make sure that they fit very snugly. They will shrink a bit as they cook, so if you start with a slightly crowded pan, you'll end up with perfect coverage. We usually make this with a mix of onion types, so there's some pretty variation in color even as they caramelize. Likewise, we call for white balsamic vinegar, as regular balsamic will darken the onions more than we like. Serve this with a crisp, sharp salad and maybe a cup of soup.

FOR THE DOUGH

1½ cups all-purpose flour

Kosher salt

8 tablespoons cold butter, cut into pieces

3 to 4 tablespoons ice water

FOR THE ONIONS

1½ pounds pearl onions

3 tablespoons butter

1 tablespoon sugar

Kosher salt

2 tablespoons white balsamic vinegar

1 tablespoon fresh thyme leaves

TO MAKE THE DOUGH, COMBINE THE FLOUR and ¼ teaspoon salt in a bowl and, using your hands or a pastry cutter, quickly work in the butter, squeezing or cutting it until the floury mixture is filled with pea-sized lumps. Drizzle 3 tablespoons ice water over the mixture and stir with your hands or a fork until it just holds together when squeezed. Add the remaining water if necessary. Gather the dough into a ball and flatten slightly, then wrap well in plastic wrap. Refrigerate for at least 1 hour and up to a couple of days.

Bring a pot of water to a boil. Drop the onions into the water and blanch for about 30 seconds. Drain well and run under cold water. When cool enough to handle, peel and trim them. Heat the butter in a heavy 10-inch skillet, preferably cast-iron, over moderately high heat. When the butter has melted and foamed, sprinkle the sugar evenly over the bottom of the pan, followed by ½ teaspoon salt. Lay the onions in the skillet and cook, without stirring, for about 8 minutes. Give the skillet a shake to jostle the onions around a bit then continue cooking until nicely browned all over, another 4 to 5 minutes. Don't worry if the onions are not fully tender; they will continue to cook in the oven. Drizzle the vinegar over the onions then scatter the thyme leaves over top. Cook, stirring occasionally, until the vinegar is reduced and syrupy, 1 to 2 minutes. Remove from the heat.

Heat the oven to 400°F. Roll out the pastry dough into an 11-inch round. Lay the pastry round directly over the onions, folding any excess dough up over the top. Bake until the pastry is golden brown, about 25 minutes. Remove from the oven and let cool in the pan for about 10 minutes. Run a knife around the edge of the skillet, then place a serving plate over the skillet and carefully invert it to unmold the tarte tatin. Don't fret if you lose any pearl onions in the transfer, simply pop them back into place. Cut into wedges and serve warm.

NOTE: If you just want some delicious glazed onions, omit the crust and simply cook the onions until they are fully tender before adding the vinegar, which should take about 10 minutes longer than noted above.

PICKLED PEARLS

MAKES ABOUT 1 PINT

The traditional garnish for a Gibson—essentially a gin martini—pickled pearl onions are a delicious treat on their own. Their piquant, bite-sized pop works well alongside a charcuterie plate or a chicken liver pâté.

1 (10-ounce) bag white pearl onions

2 strips fresh lemon zest

½ teaspoon coriander seeds

¼ teaspoon fennel seeds

6 black peppercorns

½ cup white wine vinegar

½ cup water

2 tablespoons sugar

Kosher salt

½ teaspoon dry vermouth

BRING A SMALL POT OF WATER TO A BOIL. Drop in the onions and blanch for about 3 minutes. Drain well and run under cold water. When cool enough to handle, peel the onions and trim the root ends, dropping them into a clean pint jar as you work. Tuck the strips of lemon zest into the jar.

Combine the coriander, fennel and peppercorns in a small dry saucepan and toast over moderately high heat, swirling the pan to keep them from burning, until the spices are fragrant, about 1 minute. Add the vinegar, water, sugar and 2 teaspoons salt and bring to a boil, stirring to help dissolve the sugar and salt. When the mixture is clear, remove from the heat and pour carefully over the onions. Let cool, uncovered, then stir in the vermouth and seal. Refrigerate overnight before serving. The onions will keep in the fridge for several weeks.

PINK PEARLS MAKES ABOUT 1 PINT

Another easy pickle that's less sweet and more tart, these colorful onions are great over pork chops or steak, or on the lip of a New Year's Day Bloody Mary (page 274).

Combine **1 cup red wine vinegar** with **½ cup water** in a saucepan. Add **1½ teaspoons kosher salt, ½ teaspoon sugar** and **5 black peppercorns**. Bring to a boil, stirring until the salt and sugar are dissolved. Add **1 (10-ounce) bag red pearl onions** and boil for 3 minutes. Drain, reserving the vinegar mixture. When the onions are cool enough to handle, peel and trim them, dropping them into a clean glass jar as you work. Pour the vinegar mixture over the jarred onions, seal and refrigerate overnight before serving. Like the Pickled Pearls, these will keep in the fridge for several weeks.

LAYER BY LAYER

There's nothing cuter than a pearl onion, but those good looks come with a cost—namely the time it takes to peel each one of the little buggers. Briefly boiling the onions makes the job much easier, as the outer skins loosen right up. If preparing onions to be pickled, we boil them until crisp-tender, two to three minutes. But if we know the onions will continue to cook after they are peeled, they need only to be blanched long enough to soften their outer skins, thirty seconds or so. After the onions are drained and cool enough to handle, use a paring knife to trim the root end. Often, if given a squeeze, the onion will pop through the outer layers, peeled and ready to go. Long stem ends can be a little tough to chew; we usually trim them with kitchen shears after we're done with all the peeling. Of course, all this work can be avoided if you use frozen pearl onions, though we find the texture a little lacking. Plus, we love the varieties of colors you get from using fresh pearl onions—red, gold and white—while most frozen onions seem to be white. These same rules apply when peeling cipollini onions.

BEEF STIFADO SERVES 4 TO 6

Recipes for this rich Greek stew originally caught our eye for two reasons: 1) the use of pearl onions, of course (turns out they're the perfect size for stew), and 2) the inclusion of vinegar. We love how its tang keeps the beef's richness in check. We like to serve this over buttered egg noodles, but it's also good with steamed rice, potatoes or—most interestingly—cubes of well-roasted butternut squash.

2 pounds plum tomatoes

2 pounds pearl onions

3 pounds beef chuck, cut into 2-inch cubes

2 teaspoons freshly ground allspice

Kosher salt and freshly ground black pepper

3 tablespoons olive oil

½ cup dry red wine

¼ cup red wine vinegar

1 bay leaf

1 cinnamon stick

Buttered egg noodles, for serving

BRING A LARGE POT OF WATER TO A BOIL. Drop in the tomatoes and blanch for 30 seconds; scoop out and run under cold water. Peel, chop and set aside.

Add the onions to the boiling water and blanch for 1 minute. Drain well and run under cold water. When cool enough to handle, peel and trim the onions and transfer to a bowl.

Season the beef cubes all over with the allspice, 1 tablespoon salt and several grinds of black pepper. Heat the olive oil in a large heavy pot or Dutch oven over moderately high heat. Working in batches, sear the beef until browned all over, about 5 minutes per batch. Transfer the browned meat to a dish.

Add the peeled onions to the pot and cook, stirring frequently, until browned in spots, about 5 minutes. Add the wine and cook, scraping up the browned bits from the bottom of the pot, until reduced to a thick syrup, about 4 minutes.

Add the reserved tomatoes, vinegar, bay leaf and cinnamon stick and season with salt and pepper. Return the browned beef and any juices that have collected on the plate to the pot and stir well. Bring to a boil, then cover tightly, reduce the heat to low and simmer, stirring every now and then, until the meat is very tender, about 3 hours.

If serving right away, skim off any fat from the surface of the stew. Taste and adjust the seasonings. If making ahead (like all stews, this one improves in flavor if made a day or two in advance), let the stifado cool completely, uncovered, then refrigerate overnight. Before serving, lift off and discard any solidified fat on the surface of the stew and gently reheat. Serve over buttered egg noodles.

BEEF AND ONION ANTICUCHOS SERVES 4 TO 6

The bite-sized nature of pearl onions makes them a perfect candidate for skewering and grilling. These grilled brochettes get their zing from Peruvian aji amarillo paste, a golden elixir that offers a distinctively sweet but steady heat. It's readily available online, but if you can't get your hands on it, try substituting your favorite hot sauce.

1 (10-ounce) bag pearl onions

2 plump garlic cloves

4 tablespoons extra-virgin olive oil

3 tablespoons red wine vinegar

3 tablespoons aji amarillo chile paste

½ teaspoon dried oregano

Kosher salt and freshly ground black pepper

1½ pounds flatiron or blade steak, cut into 1-inch cubes

Chopped cilantro, for garnish

BRING A POT OF WATER TO A BOIL. ADD THE onions and blanch for 2 minutes. Drain well and run under cold water. When cool enough to handle, peel and trim the onions. Set aside.

Finely grate or mince the garlic and stir it together with the olive oil, vinegar, chile paste, oregano, 1½ teaspoons salt and several grinds of black pepper in a medium bowl. Add the beef to the marinade, along with the peeled pearl onions. Stir to coat, cover with plastic wrap and refrigerate for 1 hour and up to overnight to marinate.

Heat a grill to moderately high heat. Thread the beef and onions onto 8 long skewers (if using bamboo skewers, make sure to soak them first for 30 minutes). Grill, turning occasionally, until well browned all over, 6 to 8 minutes. Remove from the heat and serve immediately, sprinkled with chopped cilantro.

LIVERS AND ONIONS SERVES 6

Kate remembers a few lonely nights during childhood, stuck at the dinner table long after everyone else had left, staring down a plate of liver and onions. Funny how time and a little life experience change everything! In this reimagining, plump chicken livers are coated in cornmeal and pan-fried until crisp and juicy, and the onions are pickled. It's a terrific one-bite appetizer, no coercion needed.

8 ounces chicken livers

½ cup all-purpose flour

1 large egg, lightly beaten

½ cup cornmeal

2 scallions, finely chopped

1 tablespoon freshly grated Parmesan

Kosher salt and freshly ground black pepper

Peanut or vegetable oil, for frying

Pink Pearls (page 238), halved lengthwise for serving

CLEAN THE CHICKEN LIVERS, CUTTING AWAY any tough or gnarly parts, including the white membranes. Cut each liver into 3 or 4 equal bite-sized pieces.

Arrange 3 shallow bowls in front of you. Place the flour in 1 bowl and the egg in another. In the third bowl, whisk together the cornmeal, scallions, Parmesan, ¼ teaspoon salt and several grinds of black pepper.

Pick up a handful of chicken livers and dredge first in the flour, then dip in the egg and then drop into the cornmeal and toss to coat lightly. Place the coated livers on a large plate and repeat with the remaining livers.

Line a large platter with paper towels. Heat about ¼ inch oil in a heavy skillet over moderately high heat until it shimmers. Working in batches, lay the chicken livers in the hot oil and fry until the undersides are golden brown, about 1½ minutes, then flip and cook until the second side is golden brown, about 1½ minutes more. The centers should be creamy and pink. Transfer to the lined platter and continue frying the remaining livers, adding more oil between batches if needed.

To serve, top each piece of liver with a pickled onion half and secure with a toothpick, if you like. Drizzle a little pickle juice over each liver and serve at once.

Cipollini. Meaning "little onions" in Italian, cipollini onions are just as suave as you'd imagine. Button-shaped and larger than pearl onions, sometimes by a hair and other times by several inches, cipollini are increasingly available in the fall and through the winter. Cipollini are very sweet, which means they take nicely to caramelizing. They can be used interchangeably with pearl onions. Some of the best known varieties are Red Marble, Bianca di Maggio and Gold Coin—so you can see that like most alliums, cipollini come in a variety of colors. Periodically, they may be labeled as Borettana onions, which harkens back to their supposed town of origin, Boretta, Italy.

CIPOLLINI AGRODOLCE MAKES ABOUT 2 CUPS

It's no surprise that the most popular way to serve these Italian onions is with a traditional Italian sweet and sour sauce. We like to use white balsamic vinegar because the onion's colors stays truer, but if you only have regular balsamic, by all means use it. This dish is satisfying on so many levels that it can almost trick us into not wanting dessert—almost!

1 pound cipollini onions

2 tablespoons olive oil

2 bay leaves

1 sprig fresh thyme or rosemary

¼ cup white balsamic vinegar

1 tablespoon sugar

Kosher salt and freshly ground black pepper

BRING A POT OF WATER TO A BOIL. DROP IN the onions and boil for 2 minutes. Drain well and run under cold water. When cool enough to handle, peel the onions and trim the root end neatly.

Heat the olive oil in a medium heavy skillet over moderately high heat. Add the onions, bay leaves and thyme and cook, stirring from time to time, until the onions are softened and nicely browned in spots, 10 to 12 minutes.

Meanwhile, combine the vinegar, sugar, ½ teaspoon salt and a few grinds of black pepper. Stir well to help the sugar and salt dissolve. Pour the vinegar mixture over the browned onions. Reduce the heat to moderate and let the mixture bubble away until the sauce is reduced and syrupy and the onions are tender, about 3 minutes. Stir the onions as needed to coat with the sauce. Remove from the heat and serve warm or at room temperature.

ROASTED ONIONS WITH WARM BACON VINAIGRETTE SERVES 6

We've always loved the sweetness and tang of warm German potato salad. Not surprisingly, those flavors work beautifully with onions, too. Sometimes we serve this salad over arugula to make it more substantial.

2 pounds mixed small onions, such as pearl onions, cipollini and/or shallots

2 tablespoons olive oil

Kosher salt and freshly ground black pepper

2 strips bacon, chopped

2 tablespoons apple cider vinegar

1 tablespoon grainy mustard

1 teaspoon sugar

1 tablespoon finely chopped flat-leaf parsley

HEAT THE OVEN TO 400°F. BRING A POT OF water to a boil. Drop in the onions and blanch for 30 seconds. Drain well and run under cold water. When cool enough to handle, peel the onions and trim the root ends, dropping the onions into a mixing bowl as you work. Add the olive oil and season with ½ teaspoon salt and several grinds of black pepper. Arrange the onions in a single layer in a medium baking dish and put in the oven. Roast until tender and lightly browned in spots, about 30 minutes.

Meanwhile, fry the bacon in a small skillet over moderately high heat, stirring from time to time, until crisp, about 8 minutes. Using a slotted spoon, scoop out the bacon and transfer to a paper towel–lined plate to drain. Keep any fat that remains in the skillet. Return the skillet to the heat and add the vinegar, mustard, sugar and ¼ teaspoon salt, stirring to dissolve the sugar. Pour the hot dressing over the roasted onions, along with the crisped bacon. Toss everything gently together, garnish with the parsley and serve warm.

SEARED DUCK WITH CIPOLLINI AND CHERRIES SERVES 4 TO 6

We love the scents of orange and cherry, juniper and allspice that waft up from the skillet as this dish cooks. They go so nicely with the mineral tang of the duck meat, but they'd taste equally good with venison, quail or even chicken thighs.

½ cup dried sour cherries

½ cup Madeira

2 large Magret duck breasts
(1½ to 2 pounds total)

2 teaspoons juniper berries

½ teaspoon allspice berries

½ teaspoon black peppercorns

Freshly grated zest and juice of 1 orange

Kosher salt

8 ounces cipollini onions

COMBINE THE CHERRIES AND MADEIRA IN A small bowl and set aside to soak while you prepare the rest of the ingredients.

Using a sharp knife, score the skin of the duck breasts in a crosshatch pattern, taking care not to cut into the flesh. Grind the juniper, allspice and peppercorns in a spice grinder, or use a mortar and pestle. Stir in the orange zest and 1 teaspoon salt. Rub the spice mixture all over the duck breasts then set aside at room temperature.

Bring a pot of water to a boil. Drop in the onions and boil for 2 minutes. Drain well and run under cold water. When cool enough to handle, peel the onions and trim the root end neatly.

Place the duck breasts skin side down in a cold heavy skillet and heat over moderate heat. Cook, without moving, until the skin is deeply browned and lots of the fat has rendered, about 8 minutes. Remove the duck and pour off most of the rendered fat. Return the duck skin side up to the skillet and continue to cook until an instant read thermometer inserted in the center of a breast reads 135°F for medium rare, 6 to 8 minutes. Transfer the duck to a plate and cover loosely with foil to keep warm.

Add the onions to the skillet and cook, stirring occasionally, until tender and browned in spots, about 8 minutes. Add the cherries and their soaking liquid and simmer until most of the liquid has evaporated, 3 to 4 minutes. Add the orange juice and simmer until the sauce is reduced and glossy, about 3 minutes more. Season to taste with salt.

Thinly slice the duck and serve with the onions, cherries and sauce.

RAMPS, SPRING ONIONS, GREEN GARLIC & GARLIC SCAPES

Ramps. Along the East Coast, the appearance of ramps, sometimes known as wild leeks, at farmers' markets means spring has sprung. We are fortunate to live in the Delaware River valley, a place where we can walk into the local woods and collect ramps ourselves—a boon in both money saved and nature explored. We also have good friends who know the woods well and are willing to share their secret ramp spots (most ramp hunters are nearly as fanatical and secretive about their stomping grounds as are mycologists).

As our friend and ramp guru Sam Marlow has taught us, it's time to start foraging when the spring ephemerals—little wildflowers like bluets, cutleaf toothwort, bloodroot and trout lilies—start popping up. As you walk, keep your eyes on the forest floor. Ramps like to grow in shaded, well-drained areas with lots of natural leaf mulch—look for their broad, pointed leaves poking through the old brown ground covering. The plants' distinctly garlicky smell may rise up to meet you if you accidentally step on them.

The tools you need are simple: a trowel, a backpack and a large plastic bag for wrapping the ramps before stowing them in your pack—this will help contain their dirt and perfume, which can linger longer than you might like. When you find a patch of ramps, there's no need to dig a hole. Just trace the root down with the trowel and loosen the dirt around the cluster of bulbs, taking care not to damage them. Early in the season, the white bulbs will be very slender and almost straight, with a very tender snap. As the season progresses, the bulbs will become larger and rounder—perfect for pickling.

Cleaning ramps well takes some time, which can add to their price at the market. But if you're foraging your own, they'll keep better with a little of the dirt still attached—just stow them, loosely wrapped in the plastic bag, in the fridge and take out what you need, washing them just before using. They'll keep for several days stored like this, though their smell may grow more pronounced over time. That's a good reminder to use them up.

POACHED EGGS WITH BUTTERY RAMPS SERVES 2

Guy loves eggs—poached, fried, sunny-side up—which is one reason why part of our backyard is now given over to a henhouse and a rotating brood of three or four chickens. We don't get nearly as many eggs as we expected to, but when the hens do deign to lay, their eggs have remarkable flavor and deep-orange, bouncy yolks. Ramps start popping up at about the same time our girls start laying more, as the days lengthen and warm up, and this is a fine way to appreciate both those special treats. And when you cook for two, you each get plenty of ramps, enough to sate your craving—at least for a little while.

1 large bunch ramps

½ teaspoon Sichuan peppercorns

3 tablespoons unsalted butter

Kosher salt and freshly ground black pepper

2 large eggs

2 thick slices of your favorite bread

WASH THE RAMPS WELL AND SHAKE DRY. Separate the greens from the bulbs (reserve the bulbs for another use, such as Pickled Ramps, page 260) and coarsely chop them. Coarsely crush the Sichuan peppercorns, using the flat side of a large heavy knife or a mortar and pestle. Bring a small pot of water to a gentle simmer and keep warm, covered.

Melt the butter in a medium skillet over moderate heat. When the butter foams, add the Sichuan peppercorns and cook, stirring, until very fragrant, about 1 minute. Add the chopped ramp greens and cook, tossing to coat in the butter, until wilted and tender, about 3 minutes. Season to taste with salt and pepper and keep warm over very low heat.

Crack each egg into a small bowl. Slide the eggs one at a time into the simmering water and poach at a bare simmer until the whites are firm but the yolks are still quite runny, about 3 minutes. While the eggs cook, toast the bread.

Put the toast on 2 plates and top each with half of the ramps, taking care to drizzle all the buttery juices over the bread. Use a slotted spoon to drain the poached eggs and lay over the ramps. Eat at once.

PICKLED RAMPS MAKE 1 PINT

Ramps are so dear that unless we manage to harvest a huge bounty, we only pickle a very small amount. For that reason, we don't process the jar but just store it in the fridge, doling out two or three pickled bulbs at a time to serve alongside sandwiches.

1 pound ramps

10 black peppercorns

1½ teaspoons gochugaru (Korean red chile flakes)

¾ cup unseasoned rice vinegar

¾ cup water

½ cup sugar

Kosher salt

CLEAN THE RAMPS WELL, THEN CUT OFF THE bottom 4 inches of the bulb and stem so they will fit neatly into a clean pint jar. Reserve the greens for another use. Add the peppercorns and gochugaru to the jar.

Combine the vinegar, water, sugar and 1 tablespoon salt in a small saucepan and bring to a boil over high heat, stirring to dissolve the sugar. Pour the boiling brine over the ramps in the jar. Seal and refrigerate overnight. Pickled ramps will keep in the fridge for several months.

PICKLED RAKKYO

Our friend Chikako made our mouths water when she told us about the pickled scallions called rakkyo she grew up eating with her Japanese parents. Fresh rakkyo are long and slender like scallions, but with clusters of egg-shaped white bulbs that looks almost like garlic cloves. Only the bulb is used when pickling. Part of a broad range of Japanese pickles collectively called *tsukemono*, jarred rakkyo are often labeled "pickled scallions" or "pickled shallots," and that confusion of terms helps describe their flavor well—the crisp bulb of a shallot with the mild sweetness of a scallion. Pickled rakkyo is often served with grilled fish, meat or rich curries, offering a contrasting sweet and sour bite. If you are lucky enough to find rakkyo at an Asian supermarket or farmers market, pickle them following the same method for the pickled ramps, substituting a thinly sliced fresh red chile for the Korean red pepper flakes.

APPALACHIAN CHIMICHURRI MAKES ABOUT 1 CUP

The Argentinean herb sauce known as chimichurri is traditionally made with parsley and lemon juice, but it's infinitely adaptable by swapping in other green herbs and acids (see below for some other ideas). All summer, we play around with as many combinations as we can think of. The herb sauce that accompanies Grilled Salmon and Spring Onions (page 267) is a variation on the theme and uses the onions' tops. We usually serve this with grilled steak, but it's also wonderful spooned over grilled chicken, lamb, fish or roasted vegetables.

1 small bunch ramps (about 3 ounces), finely chopped

1 shallot, finely chopped

⅓ cup olive oil

2 tablespoons apple cider vinegar

½ teaspoon crushed red pepper flakes

Kosher salt

COMBINE THE RAMPS, SHALLOTS, OLIVE OIL, vinegar, red pepper flakes and ½ teaspoon salt in a bowl. Stir everything together and taste; adjust the seasonings as needed. The chimichurri can be made up to 2 hours ahead.

GARLIC SCAPE CHIMICHURRI MAKES ABOUT 1 CUP

Finely chop **3 garlic scapes, 1 shallot, 1 cup parsley leaves** and **1 cup mint leaves**. Stir together with **⅓ cup olive oil, ¼ cup freshly squeezed lemon juice, ½ teaspoon Aleppo pepper** and **½ teaspoon kosher salt**. Taste and adjust the seasonings.

SCALLION AND CILANTRO CHIMICHURRI MAKES ABOUT 1 CUP

Finely chop **1 bunch scallions, 1 bunch cilantro** and **2 plump garlic cloves**. Stir together with **⅓ cup olive oil, 3 tablespoons unseasoned rice vinegar, ½ teaspoon gochugaru (Korean red pepper flakes)** and **½ teaspoon kosher salt**. Taste and adjust the seasonings.

Spring Onions. Looking like scallions on steroids, spring onions are available, as their name implies, in the late spring and into early summer. They are simply immature red, yellow or white onions that have been pulled (or thinned) early in the season to give the remaining onions more room to grow. The bulbs are sweet, tender and juicy, and we love to grill and roast them.

These thinnings are sold with their tall greens still attached, which are as deliciously edible as the small bulb attached to them. Chop the greens and use them as you would scallions in salads, marinades, salsas, pastas, what have you. Look for greens that are sprightly and unblemished. These fresh onions do not keep long. Wrap the onions loosely in plastic and store in the fridge—but plan to use them within a week.

GRILLED SALMON AND SPRING ONIONS SERVES 4 TO 6

Alaska's Copper River salmon starts hitting the market about the same time local farms start selling bunches of spring onions, and together, they are a fine way to celebrate the advent of the new season. Grilling the salmon over the trimmed onion tops protects it from the grill's heat, while offering an extra wisp of flavor.

6 to 8 spring onions

Kosher salt and freshly ground black pepper

½ cup olive oil

½ cup finely chopped flat-leaf parsley

¼ cup finely chopped dill

Finely grated zest of 1 lemon

Juice of ½ lemon

1½ pounds salmon fillets

CLEAN THE SPRING ONIONS, LOPPING OFF most of the floppy greens and setting them aside. Halve the onions lengthwise, season well with salt and pepper and toss with 2 tablespoons olive oil. Set aside.

Finely chop enough of the onion greens to measure about 2 tablespoons and transfer to a small bowl. Add the parsley, dill, lemon zest, lemon juice and ⅓ cup olive oil. Season with ½ teaspoon salt and several grinds of black pepper.

Preheat a grill to moderately high heat. Lay a large sheet of aluminum foil on a baking sheet or tray. Arrange the spring onions on one half of the foil and the reserved onion greens on the other half. Lay the salmon fillets on top of the greens, drizzle with the remaining 1 tablespoon olive oil and season well with salt and pepper.

Carefully transfer the foil and its contents to the hot grill. Grill, tossing the onions from time to time, until they are tender and the salmon is flaky, about 10 minutes. Remove from the grill and transfer the salmon and onions to a platter (discard the onion greens). Serve with the herb sauce.

ROASTED SPRING ONIONS WITH ROMESCO SAUCE SERVES 4 TO 6

In the spring in Catalonia, festivals are held to celebrate the local spring onions, called *calçots*. These slender alliums are grilled until blackened, then wrapped in sheets of newspaper and grilled some more until their hearts are perfectly tender. The idea is to peel off the blackened layers until you reach the snow-white center, then dip that in romesco sauce, a chunky mix of roasted peppers, tomatoes, garlic, chiles, hazelnuts and paprika. Our version may not be authentically Catalonian, but it's awfully good. We're always happy to have leftover romesco sauce in the fridge (this recipe will make about 2 cups worth). It's so good dolloped over roasted veggies, tucked into sandwiches and paired with fish.

FOR THE ROMESCO SAUCE

2 red bell peppers, cored

1 ripe tomatoes, cored

4 garlic cloves, unpeeled

3 tablespoons olive oil

2 dried ancho chiles

½ cup peeled hazelnuts

1 teaspoon sweet paprika

Kosher salt

2 tablespoons sherry vinegar, or to taste

FOR THE SPRING ONIONS

6 to 8 spring onions with greens attached

2 tablespoons olive oil

Kosher salt and freshly ground black pepper

TO MAKE THE ROMESCO SAUCE, HEAT THE oven to 425°F. Arrange the peppers and tomatoes in a small baking pan. Drop 2 garlic cloves in each of the peppers and drizzle 1 tablespoon olive oil into the peppers and tomato. Roast until the peppers and tomato are well caramelized but not burnt, 45 minutes to 1 hour.

Meanwhile, remove the stems and seeds from the dried chiles and slit them open so they lie flat. Toast the chiles in a small skillet over moderately high heat until softened and fragrant, about 10 seconds per side. Place the toasted chiles in a small bowl and cover with hot water, placing a small plate over the bowl to keep the chiles submerged. Soak the chiles until soft, about 15 minutes, then drain and transfer to a food processor.

Heat the remaining 2 tablespoons olive oil in the skillet over moderate heat. Add the hazelnuts and toast, stirring often so they don't burn, until golden brown, 3 to 5 minutes. Transfer the nuts and oil from the skillet to a plate to cool.

When the peppers and tomato are caramelized, remove from the oven and let them cool. Trim and clean the onions, leaving several inches of their green tops attached, then arrange them snugly in a large baking dish. Drizzle with 2 tablespoons olive oil and season well with salt and pepper. Roast until the onions are browned and tender, about 40 minutes.

Meanwhile, finish the romesco sauce. Peel the peppers, pinch off and discard the tomato skin and squeeze the roasted garlic cloves out of their skins. Add the peppers, tomato and garlic to the processor with the chiles, along with the paprika, vinegar and 1 teaspoon salt, and process until smooth. Add the nuts and pulse until the mixture just comes together but is not smooth—it should be thick and creamy while maintaining a coarse, nutty texture. Taste and adjust the seasonings, adding a bit more vinegar or salt as needed. Transfer to a bowl and serve with the roasted onions or spread some of the romesco on a shallow platter and serve the onions on top.

PIZZA WITH SPRING ONIONS AND GREEN GARLIC RICOTTA SERVES 4 TO 6

We love making pizza, and this is among the favorites that we've come up with over the years. It's allium on top of allium on top of allium! Use leftover Grilled or Roasted Spring Onions (pages 267 and 269) for this beauty, or even wedges of Salt-Baked Sweet Onions (page 116). Make **1 batch pizza dough** (see Pissaladière, page 31) and heat the oven to 500°F. Finely chop **1 head green garlic** and stir it into **2 cups ricotta**; season with **kosher salt** and **freshly ground black pepper**. Lightly **oil** a large baking sheet and stretch the dough to fill it. Spread the seasoned ricotta in a thin later over the dough. Coarsely chop however many leftover cooked spring onions you have and scatter over the ricotta. Drizzle the pizza with **1 tablespoon olive oil**. Bake until the dough is crisp and golden brown, about 15 minutes. Remove from the oven and sprinkle with **⅓ cup chopped Pickled Red Onions** (page 104) and a handful of finely chopped **chives**. Slice the pizza and serve at once.

Green Garlic & Garlic Scapes. You need not wait for garlic to fully mature to enjoy it. Like onions, garlic must be thinned in the field so that each growing bulb can reach its full potential. Those thinnings are sold as green garlic, leafy tops that lead down to a bulb that hasn't yet divided into cured garlic's distinctive cloves. Both the leaves and juicy bulb are edible, with a milder piquancy than their mature counterparts. Green garlic is one of our favorite springtime treats, and we use it as we would regular garlic, but with the knowledge that it will land a softer punch. To store, wrap green garlic loosely in plastic and refrigerate. It will keep for up to one week.

A few weeks after field thinnings, each remaining garlic plant will send up a flower stalk that loops and curls in a most picturesque way. These stalks, or scapes, need to be cut off to force more strength and resources to the growing bulb. Happily, they are also edible and can be used as you would garlic or even scallions, acting as much as a vegetable as a flavoring. We love to tuck a few scapes into a springtime bouquet—so dramatic! Unfortunately, so is their fragrance, and after a day or two, we always return them to their rightful place in the kitchen, tucked in a plastic bag and stored for several days in the fridge.

NEW YEAR'S DAY BLOODY MARYS SERVES 8

We adapted this from a V8-spattered recipe that Kate's father used to make in gigantic quantities every year for their New Year's Day open house—a true hair-of-the-dog cure-all for the festivities of the night before. In a large pitcher, stir together **6 cups tomato juice, 3 tablespoons freshly squeezed lemon juice, 1 tablespoon freshly grated horseradish root, 1 tablespoon Worcestershire sauce** and **1 tablespoon hot sauce.** Take **½ yellow onion** and juice it (as you would an orange); add the onion juice, along with **1½ teaspoons salt,** to the pitcher. Refrigerate until very cold. Before serving, stir in **1½ cups vodka** and pour into ice-filled glasses. Garnish each glass with a **Dilly Garlic Scape (page 275)** and/or **1 or 2 Pickled Pearls (page 236), Pink Pearls (page 238)** or cloves of **Italian Pickled Garlic (page 295).**

DILLY GARLIC SCAPES MAKES 1 QUART

When scapes are abundant in the summer, we preserve them as we do green beans—in a brine flavored with plenty of fresh dill and hot pepper flakes. We nibble on these with cheese and crackers, or chop them and add to salads or soups.

2 tablespoons kosher salt

3 cups room temperature water

6 fresh dill sprigs, include the flowering heads, if you have them

1 to 1½ teaspoons crushed red pepper flakes

½ teaspoon black peppercorns

8 ounces garlic scapes, trimmed

STIR THE SALT INTO THE WATER UNTIL dissolved. Set the brine aside.

Place the dill, red pepper flakes and peppercorns in a clean glass quart jar. Trim the scapes and pack them into the jar. Fill the jar with the brine solution, stopping 1 inch from the top of the jar. Fill a resealable plastic bag with water and seal; set it on top of the scapes to help submerge them in the brine.

Set the jar aside in a cool room temperature spot for 7 to 10 days. After 7 days, taste a scape. If it tastes ripe enough for your liking, seal the jar and transfer it to the refrigerator, or continue to let the scapes ferment for a few days longer until they suit your taste (they will get tangier the longer they ferment). Refrigerated, the dilly scapes will keep for several months.

GREEN GARLIC AND CHIVE MAYONNAISE
MAKES ABOUT 1½ CUPS

We readily admit to making our mayo in the food processor most of the time, but everyone should make it by hand at least once to watch and feel the emulsion come together. But it does take coordination—dribbling in oil with one hand as you mash and pound with your other is a little like rubbing your tummy while patting your head. This voluptuous golden mix is a great addition to a B.O.A.T. Sandwich (page 126).

1 bulb green garlic, finely chopped

Kosher salt

1 large egg yolk, room temperature

Juice of ½ lemon

1 teaspoon Dijon mustard

½ cup extra-virgin olive oil

½ cup grapeseed oil

1 tablespoon finely chopped chives

COMBINE THE GREEN GARLIC AND ½ TEASPOON salt in a mortar and pound to a paste with a pestle. Add the egg yolk, lemon juice and mustard and mash until thickened and sticky. Combine the olive oil and grapeseed oil in a measuring cup and start adding the oils to the garlic mixture in a slow dribble, mashing and stirring the whole time to incorporate the oil. As the mixture emulsifies, it will become thick and glossy. When all the oil has been added, taste the mayonnaise and adjust the seasonings as you like, adding a little more lemon juice or salt. Stir in the chives. Use right away, or store in a sealed container in the refrigerator for up to 3 days.

NOTE: If it's not the season for green garlic, you can substitute 3 plump cloves of regular garlic.

ANGEL EGGS

An ode to the ladies of Canal House, these beauties offer all the fun of deviled eggs, but are so much easier: Peel as many hard-boiled eggs as you like and halve them lengthwise. Spread a smear of Green Garlic and Chive Mayonnaise (above) over each egg and garnish with some chopped chives. Ta da!

GREEN GARLIC CAESAR

SERVES 4 (OR 2 HUNGRY PEOPLE WHO TRULY LOVE EACH OTHER)

Malaika Spencer, a farmer across the river in Bucks County, Pennsylvania, grows the tastiest green garlic, and we think this juicy salad is one of the finer ways to use it. A whole bulb goes into the dressing, while some of the stem is chopped and added to the croutons as they toast. The dressing needs no egg to thicken it, as the Parmesan makes it creamy enough. You could use packaged romaine hearts for this, but they are sometimes all crunch and no flavor. A good head of fresh romaine requires a little more work but tastes more alive and, well, lettuce-y. We adore the bitter edge of escarole and sometimes use that in place of romaine. When green garlic is out of season, swap in three finely chopped garlic cloves for the dressing and one thinly sliced garlic clove for the croutons.

3 slices ciabatta or country bread

1 bulb green garlic, with some of the stem

¼ cup plus 3 tablespoons extra-virgin olive oil

Kosher salt and freshly ground black pepper

6 anchovy fillets

2 tablespoons freshly squeezed lemon juice

½ cup finely grated Parmesan, plus more for garnish

1 large head romaine lettuce

HEAT THE OVEN TO 375°F. TEAR THE BREAD into rough bite-sized pieces and place on a baking sheet. Take the bottom 4 to 5 inches of the green garlic stem and halve lengthwise. Discard the woody core, if needed, and slice the stem thinly. Scatter the sliced garlic stems over the bread, along with 3 tablespoons olive oil. Season well with salt and pepper, and toss with your hands to coat evenly. Bake, shaking the pan once or twice, until the edges of the croutons are golden-brown and crisp, 10 to 12 minutes. Set aside.

To make the dressing, chop the reserved green garlic bulb. Sprinkle a generous pinch of salt over the garlic and continue to use the side of your knife to mash the garlic to a paste. Lay the anchovies over the garlic paste, chopping and mashing to incorporate. Transfer the mixture to a small bowl and whisk in the lemon juice and a few grinds of black pepper. Whisk in the remaining ¼ cup olive oil, then stir in the grated Parmesan. Taste and adjust the seasonings.

Tear away a few of the green outer leaves of the lettuce and reserve for another use. If the tops of the lettuce are very leafy and floppy, lop them off and reserve for another use—you want most of this salad to be the juicy, crunchy heart. Tear the leaves into generous bite-sized pieces and transfer to a large salad bowl.

Add the dressing to the lettuce and mix gently to coat (hands work best for this). Scrape the croutons and browned garlic bits over the salad. To finish, shave a few long strips of Parmesan over the salad and serve.

FRIED RICE WITH GARLIC SCAPES SERVES 2 TO 3

Sometimes you just need to clean out the fridge and make a quick meal. For those nights, we turn to fried rice. Stick with this basic formula, but feel free to add other leftovers as you like: bits of roast chicken, pork or steak; sautéed broccoli or mushrooms; roasted Brussels sprouts; a neglected half-full bag of frozen peas; thinly sliced celery or carrots; shredded green cabbage or kale—the fridge is your oyster. When scapes aren't in season, substitute three regular garlic cloves in their place.

3 to 4 cups cold leftover rice

2 tablespoons peanut or vegetable oil

4 garlic scapes, thinly sliced

1 bunch scallions, finely chopped

1-inch piece fresh ginger, finely chopped

Kosher salt

3 large eggs, lightly beaten

1 tablespoon soy sauce or tamari

1 teaspoon toasted sesame oil

Sriracha or chile garlic sauce, for serving

BREAK UP ANY CLUMPS IN THE RICE AND SET aside. Prep all of the other ingredients and set them up near the stove.

Heat the peanut oil in a wok or large nonstick skillet over moderately high heat. Add the scapes, scallions and ginger and fry, stirring, until vividly green and very fragrant, about 1 minute. Season with a pinch of salt. Add the rice and cook, stirring, until heated through, about 2 minutes. Push the rice and vegetables off to the edges of the wok and make a well in the center. Pour the eggs into the well and stir constantly to scramble. When the eggs are very softly set, fold them into the rice, then drizzle the soy sauce and sesame oil over all. Stir together quickly, then remove from the heat and serve immediately, preferably with sriracha or chile garlic sauce on the side.

KIMCHI FRIED RICE

Add 1 cup chopped Easiest Kimchi (page 163) along with the scapes, scallions and ginger.

ITALIAN FRIED RICE

Skip the ginger, soy sauce and sesame oil. Instead, add a big pinch of crushed red pepper flakes along with the scapes and scallions and stir in about 1 cup freshly grated Parmesan or Pecorino at the end.

GREEN GARLIC AND PANCETTA RISOTTO WITH DANDELION SALAD SERVES 4 TO 6

There comes a time every spring when a run of warm, blue-sky days convinces us it's time to shut down the furnace for the season. Invariably that very night a chill returns to the air, and when it does, we turn to risotto for comfort and warmth. Risotto is so delicious and satisfying and takes a fair amount of time and attention, so we always think of it as a main course, never a first. A lightly dressed salad of bitter greens and nuggets of fried pancetta served on top of the risotto make each bite an addictive combination of creaminess, sharpness and porky savor.

8 cups chicken stock

1 stalk green garlic

6 tablespoons olive oil

4 ounces pancetta, finely diced

1½ cups Arborio rice

1 cup dry white wine or vermouth

2 tablespoons freshly squeezed lemon juice

Kosher salt and freshly ground black pepper

1 small bunch dandelion greens

½ cup freshly grated Parmesan

2 tablespoons butter

TO MAKE THE RISOTTO, BRING THE CHICKEN stock to a gentle simmer in a saucepan and keep warm over low heat.

Remove the greens from the stalk of garlic and finely chop them; you should have about ¾ cup. Reserve the bulb for the salad.

Heat 2 tablespoons olive oil in a heavy pot over moderately low heat. Add the pancetta and cook gently, stirring from time to time, until it is crisp and its fat has rendered, 8 to 10 minutes. Use a slotted spoon to transfer the pancetta to a paper towel–lined plate to drain and set aside.

Increase the heat under the pot to moderate and add the chopped garlic greens. Cook, stirring, until wilted, about 2 minutes. Add the rice

and cook, stirring, until it is glistening all over, 1 to 2 minutes. Add the wine and cook, stirring and scraping the bottom of the pot, until mostly absorbed by the rice. Start adding the hot broth, a ladle or two at a time, give a stir and let simmer until mostly absorbed. Even if your back is turned, you can hear a change when the risotto is ready for more broth—the wet burblings and big plops will give way to a drier, steadier murmur. Continue adding broth, stirring and simmering until the rice is plump and tender and the mixture is still somewhat loose and brothy, about 25 minutes total. Try to keep a cupful of broth in reserve to stir into the risotto just before serving.

While the risotto simmers, make the salad. Finely grate or mince about half of the green garlic bulb and put it into the bottom of a salad bowl. Whisk in the lemon juice, 4 tablespoons olive oil, ½ teaspoon salt and several grinds of black pepper. Tear the dandelion leaves into bite-sized pieces and toss well with the dressing to combine.

To finish the risotto, stir in the Parmesan and butter and season to taste with salt. Add a little of the remaining broth if necessary to soften the risotto. To serve, ladle the risotto into warmed bowls and top with the salad. Sprinkle the fried pancetta over the salad and serve at once.

GRILLED FISH WITH CHARRED GARLIC SCAPE RELISH SERVES 4

While we understand the allure of smoke and hardwood fires, we are unabashed fans of gas grills. We can count on one hand the number of times we used our old charcoal grill—it always felt like such a production—but our no-frills three-burner gas job gets used year-round. Even better, it allows us to play around, like the evening we came home with a pair of fresh snapper and a handful of garlic scapes and wanted to eat now!

FOR THE RELISH

6 to 8 garlic scapes, trimmed

4 scallions, trimmed

2 celery ribs, finely chopped

½ cup pitted green olives, such as Castelvetrano, chopped

½ cup fresh mint, chopped

2 tablespoons freshly squeezed lemon juice

¼ cup olive oil

Kosher salt and freshly ground black pepper

FOR THE FISH

2 whole fish, such as snapper or branzino (1 to 1½ pounds each), cleaned

4 scallions, trimmed

1 lemon, thinly sliced

Handful of fresh mint

1 tablespoon olive oil

Kosher salt and freshly ground black pepper

TO MAKE THE RELISH, HEAT A GRILL TO moderately high. Lay the garlic scapes and scallions directly on the clean grill grates and grill, turning occasionally until softened and charred in spots, about 8 minutes. Keep the grill on.

Chop the scapes and scallions and transfer to a bowl. Stir in the celery, olives, mint, lemon juice and olive oil. Season with ¼ teaspoon salt and several grinds of black pepper. Let the relish sit at room temperature while you grill the fish.

Lay the fish on a baking sheet and stuff the cavities of each with the scallions, lemon slices and mint. Season the fish well, inside and out, with salt and pepper and drizzle with olive oil.

Lightly oil the grill grates, then lay the fish directly on the grates and grill, covered, for 6 to 8 minutes. Using a wide spatula, carefully flip the fish and continue to cook, covered, until the flesh is flaky, about 6 to 8 minutes more.

Transfer the fish to a serving platter and spoon some of the relish over the fish.

THE VITAL BULB
GARLIC

Garlic. At one time, the world was divided between joyful garlic eaters and those who looked down on them. These naysayers found the bulb—and its fragrance—coarse and offensive. But as the world grew smaller, thanks to increased immigration and easier travel, garlic became more widely (and wildly) appreciated. Indeed, whole books have been devoted to garlic, and for good reason—like onions, garlic can play so many roles, by turns fiery, mellow, sweet, golden.

There are two main subspecies of garlic. Supermarkets mostly carry soft-neck garlic because it is a good keeper and ships well. Soft-neck bulbs have skin that can range from white to pale violet, and their cloves usually grow in two concentric rings—the outer cloves are plump and generous, while the inner ones are tiny, oddly shaped and very finicky to peel. Guilty confession: We often abandon ship on these inner cloves, which feel like more trouble than they're worth.

We much prefer the hard-neck garlic that becomes available at local farms in the late summer. In these varieties—including the best-known, Rocambole—five to ten fat cloves grow in a single ring around a woody stalk. The cloves are easy to break apart and peel, and the flavor is strong and true. Hard-neck garlic doesn't have a very long shelf life, about three months, but we enjoy the heck out of it while we can. A green sprout growing up the middle of a clove is a sure sign that the garlic is past its prime, but if it's the only garlic in the house, we use it anyway, cutting the clove in half lengthwise and flicking out the green with the tip of a knife.

No matter what sort of garlic you use, keep it in a dry spot with good air circulation. Cool and dark is also good. We keep ours in a perforated ceramic bowl within easy reach on our counter. The scent of raw garlic is pervasive and does not wash off easily. Rubbing a stainless steel spoon or a cut lemon over your hands before washing them with soap and water helps somewhat.

Though it seems its heyday has passed, elephant garlic still occasionally pops up at the market. Looking like a head of garlic that has eaten its Wheaties, elephant garlic is actually more closely related to the leek, both botanically and in taste, than it is to regular garlic. Its mild onion flavor is entirely different from the sharp pungency of garlic and cannot be substituted for it.

GARLICKY GARLIC BREAD SERVES 4 TO 6

Crisp and golden on the outside, soft and buttery within, this is the garlic bread of our childhoods, and it begs to be paired with the classics—spaghetti and meatballs, baked rigatoni and eggplant parm. We like the mellowness that a few cloves of garlic confit add to the mix, but they can be omitted if you don't have them on hand.

1 loaf soft Italian bread

6 plump garlic cloves, finely chopped

3 cloves Garlic Confit (page 292), finely chopped

8 tablespoons butter

¼ cup garlic oil from Garlic Confit (page 292) or olive oil

Big pinch crushed red pepper flakes

1 tablespoon finely chopped flat-leaf parsley

HEAT THE OVEN TO 425°F. WITHOUT CUTTING completely through the bottom, cut the loaf of bread into 1-inch-thick slices. Place a large sheet of aluminum foil on a baking sheet and set the bread on the foil.

Combine the fresh garlic, the garlic confit, the butter, garlic oil (or olive oil) and a big pinch of red pepper flakes in a small skillet. Heat the mixture over moderate heat until the butter is melted, swirling the pan to incorporate the garlic. Remove from the heat and stir in the parsley. Spoon the garlicky mixture evenly between the slices of bread, using the back of the spoon to spread it to the edges of the bread as much as possible.

Gather the foil around the loaf of bread (depending on the size of your loaf, some of the top may be exposed). Bake the bread until the inside is steamy and the top is golden and crusty, about 15 minutes. Serve at once.

GARLIC TOAST MAKES AS MANY AS YOU LIKE

Make these simple toasts to serve with dishes like Steamed Clams with Shallots and Garlic (page 213) and Insalata Tropeana (page 95). They're also delicious topped with a heap of juicy Ammogghiu (page 299). Heat the oven to 450°F. Lay a **few slices of good country bread** right on the racks of the oven. Bake, keeping a keen eye on the bread so it doesn't burn, and flip it once or twice, until golden brown and toasted, about 5 minutes. As soon as you remove the toast from the oven, rub **peeled garlic cloves** over the surface of each piece of toast (one side is fine; if you want it extra garlicky, rub both sides). Drizzle the toasts with **good extra-virgin olive oil**, sprinkle with **some flaky sea salt** and serve at once.

GARLIC CONFIT

MAKES ABOUT 1 CUP GARLIC CLOVES AND 1 CUP GARLIC OIL

These buttery soft garlic cloves and deeply flavored oil add some real verve to the Garlicky Garlic Bread (page 291) and Brandade (page 309). Mash a clove or two as a quick pick-me-up for canned beans, or rub some under the skin of a chicken before roasting. Use the oil in place of regular olive oil for sautéing vegetables or searing meat.

1 cup peeled garlic cloves, from
4 to 5 heads of garlic

1 bay leaf

1 small dried red chile

1 cup olive oil

HEAT THE OVEN TO 300°F. PUT THE GARLIC cloves, bay leaf and dried chile in a small oven-proof dish and add the olive oil. Cover the dish tightly with aluminum foil and set on a rimmed baking sheet. Bake until the garlic cloves are tender when pierced with the tip of a sharp knife, about 45 minutes. Let the mixture cool completely, then transfer to a glass jar and store in the refrigerator for up to 1 month. The oil will congeal as it chills; to use, gently rewarm it to liquefy.

CLOVE AFTER CLOVE

Peeling garlic is exactly no one's favorite kitchen task, but needs must. Smashing the cloves with the flat side of a heavy knife is the most straight-forward way to go about it—the papery skins will slip right off after a good thwack. To keep the cloves intact and pretty—for instance, when making Italian Pickled Garlic (page 295)—we trim off the root end with a sharp paring knife and then use the tip of the knife to loosen the skin and peel it away. We do have friends who swear by a garlic peeler, a flexible silicone tube into which you insert a few cloves of garlic before roll-ing it back and forth across the counter, pressing down until the skins have come off. It works well enough, but our small kitchen doesn't have much space for single-use gadgets, so we stick with the knife.

If you have lots of garlic to peel, it's worth trying this trick at least once: Place the garlic cloves in a rimmed bowl and top with an inverted bowl of the same size. Hold the rims together and shake as hard as you can for about twenty seconds. It's loud and bombastic—a great way to work off frustration while doing a tedious job quickly—but it also makes a bit of a mess as those little papery skins drift out between the cracks and snow down over the counter, so you may want to take it outside. Even if all the cloves aren't perfectly peeled when you open the bowls, their skins will be loosened, making the rest of the job easy.

ITALIAN PICKLED GARLIC MAKES 1 PINT

A staple of many an antipasto bar, pickled garlic, not surprisingly, has an affinity for fresh mozzarella, briny olives and roasted red peppers. Don't be shocked if some of the garlic cloves take on a blue or greenish cast; it's simply an enzymatic reaction and is perfectly safe to eat. Older garlic may be more prone to turning blue, so when pickling, use the freshest garlic you can find.

1 cup white wine vinegar

½ cup dry white wine

6 heads garlic, cloves peeled

1½ teaspoons sugar

1 teaspoon dried oregano

½ teaspoon crushed red pepper flakes

Kosher salt

Extra-virgin olive oil, for serving

COMBINE THE VINEGAR AND WINE IN A SAUCE-pan and bring to a boil. Add the garlic cloves and boil for 1 minute. Scoop out the garlic and pack into a clean glass pint jar. Add the sugar, oregano, red pepper flakes and 1½ teaspoons salt to the vinegar mixture and return to a boil, stirring until the sugar and salt are dissolved. Pour the boiling brine over the garlic cloves to cover. Let cool, then seal and refrigerate at least 3 days before serving.

To serve, use a fork to scoop out the garlic cloves and arrange in a dish. Drizzle with some olive oil before serving.

NOTE: Once all the garlic has been eaten, save the leftover brine to use in salad dressings or as a marinade.

CHINESE PICKLED GARLIC MAKES ABOUT 1 CUP

The easiest pickle there is. We use this garlic and its very flavorful vinegar when making dipping sauces for Pork and Garlic Chive Potstickers (page 191) or savory Scallion Sesame Pancakes (page 157). To make it, peel **2 or 3 heads of garlic,** dropping the cloves into a clean half-pint jar as you work. Add enough **Chinese black vinegar** to cover the cloves and seal. Store in a cool dry place for at least 1 week before using. As with the Italian Pickled Garlic, the cloves may turn blue as they sit.

ROASTED TOMATILLO SALSA MAKES ABOUT 1 CUP

Our love for Mexican food goes deep, and we're proud to have passed that appreciation down to our son. This is the salsa he clamors for when it's taco night. A cousin to both the tomato and the cape gooseberry, tomatillos are covered by a papery husk that easily peels away to reveal a firm, green fruit. Their natural acidity makes them perfect for salsa, which we love to pair with pork tacos.

½ pound tomatillos

2 plump garlic cloves

1 jalapeño

¼ teaspoon ground cumin

Kosher salt

HEAT A BROILER TO HIGH (OR FIRE UP A grill). Line a baking sheet with foil.

Remove the husks from the tomatillos and rinse them well under warm water to remove any sticky residue. Place the tomatillos on the lined baking sheet, along with the unpeeled garlic cloves. Cut the jalapeño in half lengthwise. Remove the chile's seeds and ribs, if you like, which will make the salsa a little milder, and place the jalapeño halves on the baking sheet. Broil until the tomatillos, garlic and jalapeño are softened and blackened in spots, 5 to 8 minutes. Set aside to cool a bit.

Remove the garlic cloves from their papery skins and drop in a blender, along with the tomatillos, jalapeños and any juices that have collected on the baking sheet. Add the cumin and ½ teaspoon salt. Blend until very smooth. Refrigerate until ready to use.

VARIATIONS: Stir in some finely chopped avocado or a canned chipotle in adobo. You can stretch the salsa by adding a handful of diced white onion.

FRESH TOMATILLO SALSA MAKES ABOUT 1 CUP

If you prefer the ultra-bright flavor and color of raw tomatillos, try this version. Husk, rinse and coarsely chop **½ pound tomatillos**. Place in a blender along with **2 plump garlic cloves, 1 coarsely chopped jalapeño, ¼ cup cilantro** and **½ teaspoon kosher salt**. Blend until very smooth.

AMMOGGHIU MAKES ENOUGH FOR 1 POUND PASTA

Set high on a sloping hill that looks out to the Tyrrhenian Sea, Mary Taylor Simeti's family farm is rich in soil, history and tradition. Mary taught us this classic Sicilian sauce, which she makes a couple of times a week during the height of tomato season when it's too hot to labor long in front of the stove. It's a wonder on grilled vegetables, especially eggplant, or tossed with spaghetti. Good tomatoes make all the difference here, and the ones grown on the Simetis' land are some of the best we've ever tasted—under the intense summer sun, they develop a plummy texture and super concentrated flavor. Few of us are lucky enough to eat tomatoes grown in such a climate, but if possible, taste before you buy, or grow your own.

2 pounds ripe plum tomatoes, such as San Marzano or Roma

3 to 4 plump garlic cloves, finely chopped

⅓ cup good olive oil

½ teaspoon Aleppo pepper, or to taste

Kosher salt

1 small bunch fresh basil or parsley, finely chopped

BRING A LARGE POT OF WATER TO A BOIL, then drop in the tomatoes and blanch for about 1 minute. Use a slotted spoon to scoop out the tomatoes and transfer to a plate or bowl. (If you're planning on making pasta, keep the pot of water on the stove and reuse it, remembering to season it with salt.)

When the tomatoes are cool enough to handle, peel them and cut in half lengthwise. Use your thumb to scoop out the seeds. Neatly chop the tomato flesh and transfer it to a large bowl. Add the garlic, olive oil, Aleppo pepper and 1 teaspoon salt and stir to combine. Stir the basil into the tomatoes then taste and adjust the seasonings. The sauce can sit for a few hours at room temperature until you are ready to serve it.

ROASTED GARLIC MAKES ABOUT ½ CUP

Spread these softened cloves directly onto bread, mash them into potatoes or fold them into mayonnaise for an easy spread. Refrigerated, they will keep for a week or so.

Heat the oven to 500°F. Cut off the top ¼ inch of **2 garlic heads** to reveal the cloves. Place on a sheet of aluminum foil and drizzle with **2 tablespoons olive oil**. Wrap tightly in the foil. Roast the garlic, directly on the oven rack, until very soft, about 40 minutes.

Carefully unwrap the garlic and cool slightly, then squeeze the cloves from their papery skins.

HARISSA MAKES ABOUT 2 CUPS

Make this Tunisian spice paste once, and it's likely to become a refrigerator staple, adding deep flavor and a kiss of heat wherever it goes. Whisk a dollop into eggs when making a frittata, slick it on lamb chops before grilling, stir into beans or add some to the pot when steaming mussels or clams.

2 ounces dried guajillo chiles

2 ounces dried ancho chiles

1 teaspoon coriander seeds

1 teaspoon caraway seeds

1 teaspoon cumin seeds

6 plump garlic cloves

1 tablespoon tomato paste

Kosher salt

2 tablespoons olive oil, plus more for the jar

1 teaspoon freshly squeezed lemon juice

RINSE THE DRIED CHILES WELL, THEN TEAR off the stems and shake out the seeds. Put the chiles in a large bowl and cover with boiling water. Set a plate over the chiles to keep them submerged in the water. Soak until softened and very pliable, 30 minutes to 1 hour.

While the chiles soak, combine the coriander, caraway and cumin seeds in a small skillet and toast over moderate heat, stirring frequently, until the seeds are fragrant and turn a shade darker, about 2 minutes. Transfer the seeds to a small bowl to cool. When cooled, finely grind the spices in a spice grinder or with a mortar and pestle.

Put the garlic in a food processor and pulse until finely chopped. Using tongs, transfer the chiles to the food processor, letting the excess water drain off over the bowl first (save the soaking liquid). Add the toasted spices, tomato paste and 1 teaspoon salt. Process until the mixture is chunky and well mixed, scraping down the sides with a spatula as needed. Add the olive oil, lemon juice and 2 tablespoons of the chile soaking liquid and process until very smooth, scraping down the sides as needed.

Transfer the harissa to a jar and smooth the top. Cover with a thin layer of olive oil, seal and refrigerate until ready to use. The harissa will keep for several weeks in the fridge; add some olive oil to cover after each use.

HARISSA FRIED EGGS SERVES 1

Sure to wake you up! Heat **1 tablespoon olive oil** in a medium skillet over moderately high heat. Add **2 tablespoons Harissa** (above) and fry for about 1 minute, stirring all the while. Smear the harissa evenly over the bottom of the skillet, then crack **2 large eggs** into the skillet. Season the eggs with **kosher salt** and **freshly ground black pepper** and fry, spooning some of the oily harissa over the eggs as they cook, until the whites are set but the yolks are still runny, about 2 minutes. Serve with crusty bread or toasted pita.

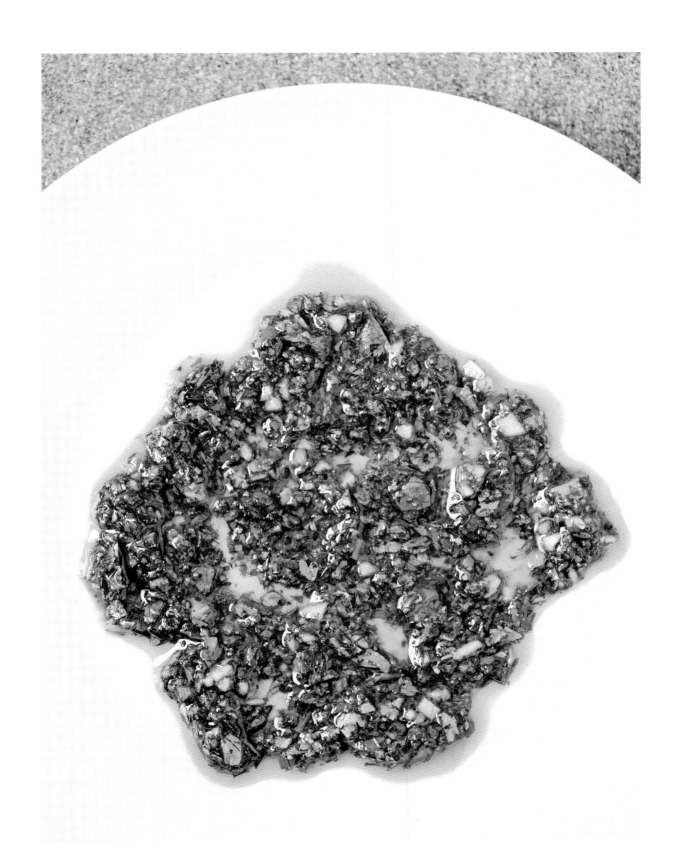

CHERMOULA MAKES ABOUT ¾ CUP

This North African sauce is extremely versatile—it can be used either as a marinade (see Grilled Lamb Chops Two Ways, page 304) or as a last-minute seasoning (Braised Lamb Shanks with Chermoula, page 59). We like to drizzle it over a swirl of hummus or toss it with roasted carrots or cauliflower as soon as they come out of the oven—the aroma of the herbs and spices will bloom throughout your kitchen. It's also a natural over roast chicken or fish. Because the herbs tend to blacken over time in the lemon juice, chermoula is best used soon after it is made, but it can be made a few hours ahead and refrigerated with a piece of plastic wrap laid directly over the sauce.

2 teaspoons cumin seeds

½ teaspoon coriander seeds

1 teaspoon sweet paprika

½ teaspoon Aleppo pepper

¼ cup freshly squeezed lemon juice

Kosher salt

¼ cup olive oil

4 plump garlic cloves

1½ cups fresh cilantro

1½ cups fresh parsley

1 teaspoon red wine vinegar

COMBINE THE CUMIN AND CORIANDER SEEDS in a small dry skillet and toast over moderately high heat until fragrant, about 1 minute. Remove from the heat and let cool, then grind finely in a spice grinder or with a mortar and pestle. Transfer the toasted spices to a bowl along with the paprika, Aleppo pepper, lemon juice and ¾ teaspoon salt. Whisk everything together until the salt is dissolved, then whisk in the olive oil.

Coarsely chop the garlic, then add a handful of the cilantro and parsley to the cutting board and chop together with the garlic. When broken down, add another handful and chop, continuing this way until all the herbs have been added and everything is very finely chopped. Stir the herbs and garlic into the lemon juice mixture. Stir in the vinegar, then taste and adjust the seasoning.

CARROTS WITH CHERMOULA SERVES 4 TO 6

Heat the oven to 400°F. Cut **1 pound carrots** into chunks. Toss the carrots with **2 tablespoons olive oil, 1 teaspoon kosher salt** and **several grinds of black pepper**. Spread out on a baking sheet and roast until the carrots are browned and tender, about 25 minutes. Dollop **3 tablespoons Chermoula** (above) over the roasted carrots and toss to coat.

GRILLED LAMB CHOPS TWO WAYS

One day we had a package of beautiful lamb chops in the fridge, as well as a freshly made batch of chermoula and a more seasoned jar of harissa. We seasoned all of the chops with salt and pepper, then painted half of them with a thin layer of harissa and threw the rest in the chermoula to marinate overnight. The next day we grilled them to medium rare, about 3 minutes per side over high heat. Then we went back and forth, eating a chermoula chop, then a harissa one, licking our fingers and diving in for another, completely undecided as to which we loved more. We enjoy that delicious indecision, so now we always make both kinds.

CINNAMON ONIONS SERVES 4 TO 6

Spiced with harissa, lemon and cinnamon, these juicy onions make a fine accompaniment to Hrous-Spiced Chicken Meatballs (page 55), but are also delicious folded into a lamb gyro or paired with grilled merguez sausages. Heat **1 tablespoon olive oil** in a medium heavy skillet over high heat. Add **4 thinly sliced yellow onions** and fry, stirring from time to time, until browned in spots and crisp-tender, about 3 minutes. Stir in **2 teaspoons freshly grated lemon zest, 2 tablespoons freshly squeezed lemon juice, 2 teaspoons Harissa (page 300), ½ teaspoon ground cinnamon** and **½ teaspoon kosher salt**. When everything is well combined, remove from the heat and taste, adding a little more salt or lemon juice as needed.

BASIL PESTO MAKES ABOUT 1 CUP, ENOUGH FOR 1 POUND PASTA

It takes surprisingly less time to make pesto by hand than you might think. You may spend the first two minutes grumbling that the job will take forever, but suddenly the basil softens and collapses under the pounding pestle, and in a few more minutes you're holding the most beautiful jade green sauce and your whole kitchen smells fantastic. A food processor may seem faster, but cleaning all those moving pieces tacks time on the back end. Most pestos call for pine nuts, but we usually reach for almonds since we always have them on hand. Slivered almonds are the easiest to use, but raw whole almonds work fine, producing a slightly earthier blend.

2 plump garlic cloves

2 tablespoons slivered almonds, lightly toasted

Kosher salt and freshly ground black pepper

2 cups loosely packed basil leaves

½ cup olive oil

½ cup freshly grated Parmesan or Pecorino Romano

Finely grated zest of 1 lemon

COMBINE THE GARLIC, ALMONDS, ½ TEASPOON salt and a few grinds of black pepper in a large mortar. Grind together with the pestle until smashed and broken down. Add the basil and half of the olive oil and continue to grind, stir and mash—a process that will take several minutes— until the basil and nuts are completely broken down and finely mashed. Stir in the cheese, lemon zest and remaining olive oil then taste and adjust the seasonings. If you aren't using the pesto right away, cover it with a thin film of olive oil, which will help keep it from discoloring, and refrigerate it for up to 2 days. We have frozen pesto with great success—a joy to discover in the frigid depths of January.

VARIATION
Replace some or all of the basil with a combination of fresh parsley and mint and add a pinch of crushed red pepper flakes.

BRANDADE MAKES ABOUT 3 CUPS

Guy's family celebrates Christmas Eve with a feast of the seven fishes, and this dish has worked its way into the rotation along with more traditional lobster sauce, fried salt cod (or *bacala*, as they call it) and eel. We serve it with crostini as an appetizer. The unbaked brandade freezes well, so sometimes we make a larger batch and parcel it out into small ramekins for future parties. Around the holidays, we often place the cod in a large Tupperware container and set it outside to soak, rather than take up valuable fridge space.

1 pound salt cod

2 sprigs fresh thyme

1 bay leaf

10 black peppercorns

3 cups whole milk

1 pound Yukon gold potatoes

Kosher salt

4 cloves Garlic Confit (page 292)

¼ cup garlic oil from Garlic Confit (page 292)

Toasted bread, for serving

PUT THE SALT COD IN A LARGE BOWL AND cover with cold water. Put the salt cod in the refrigerator and let soak for 24 hours, changing the water 2 or 3 times. At the end of the soaking time, the fish should feel almost fresh again and taste just pleasantly salted.

Drain the fish and place it on a cutting board. Run your fingers over the flesh and pull out any pin bones that you come across. Cut the fish into evenly sized chunks and place in a deep saucepan, along with the thyme, bay leaf and peppercorns. Pour the milk over the fish to cover. Bring to a simmer over moderately high heat, then reduce the heat to moderately low and cook, uncovered, at a very gentle simmer until the fish flakes apart very easily, about 25 minutes. Let cool for a few minutes in the milk mixture.

Meanwhile, peel the potatoes, cut into 1-inch chunks and place in a pot of cold salted water. Bring to a boil over high heat, then reduce the heat and simmer until the potatoes are very tender, about 20 minutes. Drain well and transfer to a large bowl.

Heat the oven to 400°F. When the fish is cool enough to handle, use your hands to separate it into small flakes and drop into the bowl of potatoes (reserve the milk, discarding the herbs and peppercorns). Add the garlic confit cloves and the garlic oil. Using an electric mixer or a potato masher, mash the fish, potatoes, garlic and oil together until very well combined, adding ½ to 1 cup of the reserved milk from the skillet to help smooth out the mixture. If you want a smoother brandade, run the mixture through a food mill. Transfer the brandade to a small, lightly oiled gratin dish (or three or four small ramekins), smoothing the top.

Bake the brandade until hot and golden brown on top, about 20 minutes. Serve with toasted bread.

GRACE'S PICKLED EGGPLANT
MAKES 6 TO 7 QUARTS

One day, while our boys were at soccer practice, our friend Grace quietly slipped a jar of homemade pickled eggplant to Guy. She knew we had lived in Sicily and that Guy loved eggplant. One bite of these juicy, oily preserves and we were hooked. We badgered Grace to teach us, and a year later we finally spent a couple of days together in our studio. It was quite an endeavor, but with three of us working side by side, the work passed easily. The eggplant is preserved three ways—with salt, with vinegar and with oil, and we like to eat it with cheese and plenty of crusty bread to soak up the garlicky juices. This recipe makes an insane amount, but you'll be happy to have it on hand all winter or to share with to a friend.

25 pounds eggplant

3 pounds kosher salt

1 gallon white distilled vinegar

3 quarts water

1 gallon extra-virgin olive oil

4 heads garlic

8 jalapeños

Dried oregano

TRIM AND PEEL THE EGGPLANTS. CUT THE peeled eggplant into slender, French fry–like strips by first cutting the eggplant in half crosswise, then cutting each half lengthwise into planks and finally cutting each plank into strips. If you have a mandoline that cuts French fries, you can use that.

As you cut the eggplant, lay them in a deep pot, generously sprinkling each layer with salt (for this amount of eggplant, you should use the whole 3 pounds of salt). You may have to divide the eggplant between a few pots. Set another pot or narrow bowl on top of each pot and add weights to help compress the eggplants and release their water, which improves their texture. Grace likes to use bricks wrapped in plastic wrap, or big cans of tomatoes. Set aside to sit overnight, but check on them periodically—the eggplants will release lots of water, which may overflow the pot. Be ready to bail out some of the liquid, if necessary.

The following day, drain the eggplants, which will have shrunk considerably, and start wringing them out with your hands. Take a handful of eggplants and squeeze as hard as you can over the sink. This will take some time and muscle. Transfer the squeezed eggplants to a bowl as you work.

Meanwhile, combine the vinegar and water in a large wide stockpot and bring to a boil over high heat. When the vinegar mixture has come to a boil, set up 3 or 4 large sheet pans. Working in batches, add the eggplants to the boiling vinegar and cook until plumped but still firm, 4 to 6 minutes. Use a large sieve to scoop out the eggplants, letting the vinegar drain back into the pot, then spread out on the sheet pans to cool a bit.

When all the eggplants have been cooked, drizzle each batch with olive oil, just enough to coat them. Divide the garlic and jalapeños evenly over each batch and sprinkle with plenty of dried oregano. Using your hands, toss the mixture together gently, then pack it into an assortment of clean glass jars, stopping when each is halfway full. Add olive oil to cover, then continue to pack in the eggplant to the top, adding more olive oil to cover. Let the olive oil settle into the jars for about 30 minutes, then add more olive oil as needed to each to make sure the eggplants are fully covered. Seal the jars and store at cool room temperature for at least 3 days before serving. They will keep for a couple of months in a cool dark place. If you open a jar and don't eat all of it in one go, refrigerate the remainder, but let it come to room temperature before serving.

GARLICKY BROCCOLI RABE SERVES 6

We don't question our son's abiding love for bitter greens, but it does make Guy glow with pride. This recipe is for broccoli rabe, but we use the same technique and proportions for regular broccoli, green beans, kale, cauliflower, carrots—really, almost any vegetable. Often we make this garlicky tumble of greens just so they can be tucked into a grilled provolone sandwich. They are also delicious forked into a chewy roll with some leftover Cuban Pork Roast (page 323).

Bring a large pot of water to a boil. While you wait for the water to boil, trim the tough ends of **2 bunches broccoli rabe** and discard. Salt the water well, then add the broccoli rabe and cook for 5 minutes. Remove from the heat and drain well. Let the broccoli rabe sit in a colander until cool enough to handle. Chop the broccoli rabe (coarsely if serving it as a side dish; finely if you're adding it to a sandwich). Finely chop **8 to 10 plump garlic cloves**. Heat **¼ cup olive oil** in a large heavy skillet over moderate heat. Add the garlic and cook, stirring, until very fragrant, about 2 minutes. Add the broccoli rabe and toss to coat with the oil and garlic. Season with **salt** and a **pinch of crushed red pepper flakes**, if you like. Cook, stirring from time to time, until the broccoli rabe is very tender, 8 to 10 minutes.

SPAGHETTI WITH PISTACHIOS, GARLIC AND MINT SERVES 4

During a chance meeting at a local coffee shop, an acquaintance mentioned in passing a pasta his grandmother used to make—all we remember hearing is "pistachios, garlic and mint." But it stuck in our heads, and we couldn't wait to play with it. Now this dish has become our new *aglio e olio*, an instant pantry classic. The saffron adds an interesting depth and perfume, but don't sweat it—the spaghetti will still be delicious without it.

1 pound spaghetti

⅓ cup olive oil

1 cup shelled pistachios, coarsely chopped

Kosher salt

4 plump garlic cloves, finely chopped

½ teaspoon saffron threads

¼ teaspoon crushed red pepper flakes, or to taste

1 large bunch fresh mint, finely chopped

BRING A LARGE POT OF WELL-SALTED WATER to a boil and cook the spaghetti in the boiling water until almost tender.

Meanwhile, heat the oil in a large skillet over moderately high heat. Add the pistachios and cook, stirring, until nicely browned, 1 to 2 minutes. Use a slotted spoon to scoop out the pistachios and transfer to a plate to cool and crisp. Season them with salt.

Return the skillet of oil to the stove, reduce the heat to moderately low, and add the garlic, saffron and red pepper flakes. Cook the garlic until softened and very fragrant, about 2 minutes. Keep warm over very low heat until the spaghetti is ready to add to the skillet.

Using tongs, transfer the cooked spaghetti from the pot to the skillet. Add the mint and a cupful of the pasta cooking water, turn up the heat to moderately high, and cook the spaghetti in the garlicky oil, tossing with the tongs, until the pasta is al dente and cloaked in a lustrous sauce. Add a little more pasta cooking water as needed to thin the sauce.

Divide the pasta among bowls or plates and top each serving with a generous handful of pistachios.

PIZZA ESCAROLE SERVES 6 TO 8

Pronounced "pizza shcarole" by Guy's New Jersey family, this filled pizza is a family treasure. Guy's great-grandmother, grandmother, Aunt Aggie and Aunt Eloise were all revered for their renditions, and we're proud to carry on the tradition. The pizza's thin crust should be absolutely bursting with escarole and seasoned heavily with anchovies and black olives. An important note: Make sure the escarole is completely cooled before spreading it over the dough—if it's too warm, the crust may become gummy.

3½ cups all-purpose flour

¾ teaspoon active dry yeast

Kosher salt

1½ cups warm water

2 large heads escarole

2 tablespoons olive oil, plus more for oiling the pan

2 to 4 plump garlic cloves, finely chopped

½ cup black olives, pitted and coarsely chopped

Pinch of crushed red pepper flakes

2 (2-ounce) cans anchovies packed in oil

TO MAKE THE DOUGH, WHISK TOGETHER THE flour, yeast and 1 teaspoon salt in a large bowl. Add the water and stir until a shaggy dough comes together. Turn the dough out on to a floured board and knead until it is bouncy and smooth, about 8 minutes. Shape the dough into a ball, place in a large, lightly oiled bowl, cover with plastic wrap and let rise until doubled in size, at least 1 hour.

While the dough is rising, bring a large pot of water to a boil. Wash the escarole well, shake off the excess water from the leaves and coarsely chop them. When the water boils, add the lighter inner leaves first and cook for 1 minute before adding the remaining dark green outer leaves (you don't need to be fanatical about separating the leaves, but this does help them cook evenly). Boil for 2 minutes, then drain well.

Heat 2 tablespoons olive oil in a large skillet over high heat. Add the drained escarole and cook, tossing with tongs, until tender, 3 to 5 minutes. Season with 1 teaspoon salt, toss well and transfer to a bowl to cool.

When the escarole has cooled completely and the dough is risen, heat the oven to 450°F. Generously oil a large baking sheet, using your hands so they are good and oily. Cut off about ⅔ of the dough and stretch it to make a very thin crust that covers the bottom of the baking sheet and up the sides. Guy's family recommends lifting and pulling the dough rather than pushing it; if the dough tears or gets holes, simply pinch off a piece of dough and patch it.

Spread the cooled escarole evenly over the dough, making sure to cover it completely. Sprinkle the garlic, olives and crushed red pepper flakes over the escarole. Tear the anchovies into smaller pieces and dot evenly over the filling; drizzle the oil from the anchovy cans over everything.

Take the remaining dough and stretch it enough to cover the top of the pizza. This is easiest to do by holding it from the top and letting the weight of the dough pull itself down and do much of the work for you. Don't worry if the dough tears a bit. Lay the dough over the escarole and pull the bottom edges up and over to seal it. Drizzle some oil over the top and spread it lightly with your hands. Place in the oven and bake until the crust is golden brown, about 25 minutes. Remove from the oven and let cool slightly before cutting into squares.

CAMARONES AL MOJO DE AJO

SHRIMP IN GARLIC SAUCE SERVES 4 TO 6

When we lived in Santa Fe, we ordered this dish ad nauseam from a neon-lit Mexican restaurant on the city's south side. We were powerless in the face of this garlicky, tangy tangle of shrimp. After we moved away, we used to daydream about that *mojo de ajo*, and every trip back included at least one visit to get our fill. Is devastated too strong a word when we discovered that the restaurant closed? After a suitable mourning period, we set to work and came up with this ridiculously easy version. Once the shrimp are peeled and the garlic is chopped, it comes together in a flash.

2 pounds medium shrimp

1 large head garlic, cloves finely chopped

⅔ cup freshly squeezed lime juice

¼ teaspoon crushed red pepper flakes

Kosher salt

2 tablespoons olive oil

2 plum tomatoes, cored and finely chopped

2 tablespoons finely chopped cilantro

Steamed white rice, for serving

PEEL AND DEVEIN THE SHRIMP, MAKING SURE to remove the tail shell. Give the shrimp a rinse under cold water, then place in a nonreactive bowl. Add the garlic, lime juice, red pepper flakes and 1 teaspoon salt to the shrimp. Toss everything together and marinate in the fridge for 20 minutes.

Heat a heavy skillet over high heat. Add the olive oil then, using a slotted spoon, scoop out the shrimp and as much garlic as you can from the bowl and add to the hot pan. Cook the shrimp without stirring for 1 minute, then add the tomatoes, give everything a stir and cook until the shrimp are pink and cooked through, about 1 minute more. Remove from the heat and stir in the chopped cilantro. Taste and adjust the seasonings. Serve the warm shrimp over steamed white rice.

CUBAN PORK ROAST SERVES 8 TO 10

Rubbed with a garlicky mojo and slow-roasted, this recipe is our hands-down favorite way to eat pork. It's terrific party food, served with a big pot of Black Beans (page 79) and rice. Any leftovers get tucked into Cuban sandwiches (see below) or chopped coarsely and fried in a dry heavy skillet until the outside of the meat is golden and crusty. We fold warm tortillas around these porky nuggets—similar to carnitas—and top with Tomatillo Salsa (page 296). If you can't find sour oranges, substitute ½ cup each freshly squeezed lime juice and orange juice.

8 sour oranges

1 large head garlic, cloves finely chopped

1 tablespoon dried oregano

1 tablespoon ground cumin

Kosher salt and freshly ground black pepper

1 (7- to 8-pound) boneless pork butt or pork shoulder

JUICE THE SOUR ORANGES; YOU SHOULD have about 1 cup juice. Measure out ¼ cup of the juice and transfer to a small bowl. Cover and refrigerate the remaining juice.

Whisk the garlic, oregano, cumin, 1 tablespoon salt and 2 teaspoons freshly ground black pepper into the small bowl of sour orange juice. Using the tip of a sharp paring knife, make 1-inch-deep slits all over the pork. Rub the garlicky mixture over the pork, pushing it into the slits with your fingertips. Set the pork in a roasting pan, cover tightly with plastic wrap, and refrigerate overnight to marinate.

Remove the pork from the refrigerator about 1 hour before it goes in the oven. Heat the oven to 350°F. Remove the plastic wrap and pour the remaining sour orange juice plus ½ cup water around the pork. Roast, basting every 30 minutes or so, until the pork is tender and crowned by a well-browned crust. An instant-read thermometer inserted in the center of the pork should register about 155°F. This should take 2½ to 3 hours.

Remove the pork from the oven and transfer it to a large cutting board; cover it loosely with foil to keep warm. Pour the cooking juices from the pan into a small saucepan, scraping in any browned bits from the pan. Ladle off the fat and warm the sauce over moderate heat. Taste and adjust the seasonings.

To serve, slice the pork thinly and serve with the sauce.

FRESH CUBAN SANDWICH SERVES 4 TO 6

Honestly, it's worth making the Cuban pork roast just for these sandwiches. Split **1 baguette** lengthwise, keeping it attached, and spread open on a cutting board. Lavishly spread one side of the baguette with **mayonnaise**; spread the other side with **Dijon mustard**. Lay thin slices of the **Cuban Pork Roast** (above) over the bottom of the loaf, moisten with some of the cooking juices, and top with plenty of **Citrus-Pickled Onions** (page 104). Close up the baguette and let sit for at least 1 hour (if you can!) for the flavors to meld, then cut into smaller sandwiches before serving.

DIY BLACK GARLIC

If you love black garlic, it's worth making it yourself, and it's easy enough to do. We have made it using a small rice cooker, bought expressly for this purpose, as a faint but stubborn aroma of garlic will linger in the machine long after the experiment is over. Set the cooker on the "keep warm" setting and arrange as many heads of garlic as will fit in one layer on the bottom of the pot. Cover and set aside, leaving it on the warm setting. After 7 days, start checking the garlic to see if it is ready. Depending on your machine and how much garlic you are making at once, it will take 7 to 14 days for the cloves to soften, blacken and become tar-like. They should mash easily under a fork's pressure. Once the cloves have reached the state of black gold that you want, remove them from the rice cooker, let cool, then transfer to a resealable plastic bag and store in the fridge, where they will keep for several weeks.

BLACK GARLIC SPREAD MAKES ABOUT ½ CUP

A great introduction to using black garlic, this appetizer spread couldn't be easier. Working in a small bowl, mash together **4 ounces cream cheese, 4 black garlic cloves, 1 tablespoon chopped chives, 1½ teaspoons grated horseradish, ½ teaspoon finely grated lemon zest, ¼ teaspoon kosher salt** and several grinds of **black pepper**. Serve with stoned wheat crackers.

BLACK IS THE NEW BLACK

Black garlic has become incredibly trendy quite quickly. Often misidentified as fermented, black garlic's distinctively inky cloves actually develop thanks to a slow-motion Maillard reaction. Instead of browning quickly over high heat, the whole unpeeled bulbs are aged in a warm, humid environment until the cloves become black and sticky, a process that takes a few weeks. After this transformation, the garlic is virtually unrecognizable as such—its sharpness and bite have given way to notes of prune, molasses and balsamic vinegar. Unsurprisingly, chefs love this umami-rich ingredient.

One of the easiest ways to appreciate the unique flavor of black garlic is to mash a few cloves into a stick of butter and use it as a compound butter melted over grilled steak. You can also use it as you would regular garlic—whisked into vinaigrette, say—but the flavor profile will be deeper, richer and more bittersweet. Black garlic is becoming readily available but if you have a rice cooker and a few weeks on your hands, you can easily and cheaply make your own.

EGGPLANT SALAD WITH BLACK GARLIC TAHINI DRESSING SERVES 4 TO 6

Layers of tahini, lemon, toasted spices, fresh herbs and tart fruit—the inspiration could only come from Ottolenghi. Garlic and tahini are natural partners, and black garlic adds an almost chocolatey depth to the alliance. Charring the eggplant produces flesh that is smoky and silky, but if you don't want to go to the trouble, this dressing works just as well on planks of roasted eggplant and zucchini.

3 medium eggplants

4 cloves black garlic

½ cup well-stirred tahini

½ cup water

¼ cup freshly squeezed lemon juice

Rind from ½ preserved lemon

Kosher salt

2 teaspoons sesame seeds

1 teaspoon cumin seeds

½ teaspoon ground sumac

⅓ cup pomegranate seeds

1 tablespoon finely chopped flat-leaf parsley

Toasted pita, for serving

ROAST THE EGGPLANTS DIRECTLY OVER THE grates of a gas stove over moderately high heat, turning as needed with tongs, until they are charred all over, tender and beginning to slump and collapse, 10 to 15 minutes. This will smell wonderful, but it will also make a mess as the eggplant juices drip and caramelize onto your stovetop. (For a little less cleanup, you can do this on a grill.) Transfer the eggplants to a colander set over a bowl and let cool.

Combine the black garlic, tahini, water, lemon juice, preserved lemon rind and 1 teaspoon salt in a blender. Blend until very smooth.

Combine the sesame and cumin seeds in a small skillet and cook over moderate heat, swirling the skillet to keep the seeds from burning, until lightly toasted and fragrant, about 1 minute. Remove from the heat and transfer the seeds to a small bowl.

Carefully remove the skin from the eggplants and tear the flesh into long strips, discarding any big pockets of seeds, and arrange the strips on a serving platter as you work. Drizzle the tahini dressing over it. Sprinkle the toasted sesame and cumin seeds and the sumac over the dressing. Scatter the pomegranate seeds and parsley over everything and serve with toasted pita.

INDEX

THANKS

MANY PEOPLE GATHERED AT OUR TABLE, both literally and figuratively, to help make this idea become reality, and we can't thank them enough.

First off, without Diane Abrams, former colleague and forever friend, we might never have started on this road in the first place. A simple "I know you can do it" from Diane is worth more than gold, and we know to listen when she says, "Why not try this?"

Obviously, it pays to be friends with good cooks. Some of our favorite recipes in this book were adapted from ones shared by Christine Ambrosino, Sylvie Baumgartel, Patricia Blake, Agnes Burke, Paul Grimes, Cheryl Alters Jamison, Dan Kaplan, Franky Kong and Jenni Kim, Fabrizia Lanza, Deborah Madison, Naomi Mobed, Giovanna Pacino, Grace Reading, John Roach, Stephanie Schneider, Barton Seaver, Mary Taylor Simeti, Zanne Early Stewart and Josh Thomsen.

And then there are the friends and family all over the country who cooked from this book, texted us photos and offered thoughtful tasting notes and suggestions. Stephen Beili, Becca Brown, Lynn Cline, Edie Dillman and Jonah Stanford, Andy Dudzik, Erinn Hade Craigmile, Michael and Jennifer Graziano, CJ Higley and Brook Vinnedge, Jenn Murkli and Christopher Gifford, Christine Weiss, Clementine Wood, Carmel Wroth and Connie Yun—we owe you!

Recognizing that not everyone in this country has easy access to good, fresh food, we feel very blessed to live in a small town where we do. In addition to a very good supermarket—ShopRite in Flemington, New Jersey—we rely on a number of amazing small farms and markets on both sides of the Delaware River, including Roots to River Farm, Gravity Hill Farm, Nonesuch Farm Market and Homestead Farm Market. Little Lake Orchard, our cousins' farm in Vermont, keeps us in pork throughout the year. Another local farmer and friend, Sam Marlow, generously shared her favorite foraging spots and know-how with us.

Not surprisingly, a deep number of cooks, writers, artists and other creative, food-minded people are also drawn to this area. Canal House's Christopher Hirsheimer and Melissa Hamilton, Ian Knauer and Shelley Wiseman of The Farm Cooking School, Poor Farm Food's Robin Hollis and Douglas Piccinnini, Jill and Stephen McDonnell and the whole Asoudegan family—thank you for making this little corner of the world ever more delicious and inspiring.

The Burgess Lea and Quarto teams have been a dream to work with. Thanks to Janet Teacher, Alyssa DeCarlo and Raquel Pidal for their meticulous and thoughtful editing that allowed our particular voice to come through. We have long admired Jan Derevjanik's clean and elegant cookbook designs, and we pinched ourselves when we learned she would be designing our own. We couldn't be happier. Thanks to Ken Newbaker for patiently listening to all our suggestions (and implementing so many of them!), and to YC Media for helping to put us on the map. Our friend Kendra Thatcher keeps a steady eye on our social media comings and goings, giving us a gentle nudge when we've disappeared into the real world for too long.

Finally, one night we were having dinner with our good friend Andrew Nowick, who listened quietly as we worried about finishing this book on time. The next morning, he sent a note saying, "So I'm wondering whether you might wanna boss me around for the fall?" And just like that, everything fell into place. Andrew tested most of the recipes in these pages, offered keen and critical feedback, kept the kitchen humming, made us laugh, fed us dinner, watched our kid and doubled as a hand model. What more could we ask for?